Dear Student,

Sicher in Grammatik is an advanced workbook for students of English who want to revise what they have already learnt during their earlier years at school.

It combines a summary of the most important rules of English grammar with exercises designed to help you to avoid making mistakes so you can face English tests more confidently.

The workbook comprises eleven chapters containing structures that you regularly come across when reading English texts, doing homework or preparing for tests. The sections are arranged in a way that underlines and characterises their function: Talking about the present, Describing, etc.

The individual chapters are divided into **basic rules** and **exercises**.

The **basic rule**s explain the grammatical structures in simple English and demonstrate the use of certain points of grammar through contextualized examples that are communicative and easy to remember. You'll also find excerpts from English literature (Nick Hornby, George Orwell) or newspaper articles that exemplify how particular structures are used.

The **exercises** follow the **basic rules**, starting with relatively straightforward exercises and going on to more demanding ones later on. While the easier exercises have been designed to test your basic knowledge of structures, the more challenging ones will help you to improve your skills at text production. Each exercise contains a reference to the **basic rules** section which deals with the grammatical structures the exercise practises (→ A, B ...).

You'll also find a number of **Tips** next to the rules and some of the exercises. These tips give extra information, highlight stylistic variations, or warn you about particular traps and trouble spots.

We don't advise you to go through the book chronologically from cover to cover. It would be better to concentrate on the areas of grammar you're not quite sure of and tend to make mistakes in. If you want to revise certain structures on your own, try looking at some recent English tests or homework that your teacher has corrected and make a list of the most common mistakes. If, for example, you're not sure when to use the past tense and when to use the present perfect, you can turn to the relevant section in *Sicher in Grammatik*. The **list of grammatical terms** (p. 100) contains an overview of important grammatical terms. The relevant chapter numbers are given for all terms dealt with in this book.

Whether you read the basic rules before tackling the exercises or whether you go straight to the exercises is up to you. Make sure you look at the suggested solution to check your results, which you will find on the CD at the back of the book. If you discover that you are making mistakes, go back to the basic rules and try to find out where you have gone wrong.

We hope that you will enjoy working with *Sicher in Grammatik* and that it will help you to do well in your final exams.

Your **Abi Workshop** Team

1 Talking about the present

- **A** The simple and the progressive form of the present 4
- **B** Dynamic verbs and stative verbs 5
- **C** The present tense sequence 8

2 Talking about the past

- **A** The past tense 12
- **B** The present perfect 14
- **C** Related tenses 18
- **D** The past tense sequence 19

3 Talking about the future

- **A** Different tenses to express future meaning 24
- **B** Basic future tenses 24
- **C** Other future forms 28

4 Using modal auxiliaries

- **A** Modal auxiliaries and their meanings 34
- **B** Modal auxiliaries and their substitutes 35
- **C** Equivalents of German 'sollen' 39

5 Using the passive

- **A** Active and passive voice 42
- **B** Forms of the passive 42
- **C** The use of the *by-agent* in passive sentences 43
- **D** Verbs with two objects in passive sentences 45

6 Using indirect speech

- **A** Indirect speech with tense shift 48
- **B** Indirect questions and commands 49

7 Linking ideas

A	Forming complex sentences	54
B	Sentences with adverbial clauses	55
C	Sentences with relative clauses	57
D	Conditional sentences	60
E	Linking sentence parts with gerunds and participles	63

8 Describing

A	Adjectives and adverbs	70
B	Special cases	70
C	The position of adverbs and adverbials in the sentence	73

9 Choosing the right non-finite verb form

A	The infinitive	78
B	The gerund	83
C	The participle and the infinitive after verbs of perception	86

10 Using the articles

A	The definite article	90
B	The indefinite article	91
C	The position of the articles	92

11 Using stylistic devices

A	Inversion	96
B	Emphasis	96
C	The *there* construction	97

Appendix

Grammatical terms	100
Irregular verbs	102

Talking about the present

A The simple and the progressive form of the present

The **present** is a very important tense, for your oral as well as for your written work.

You use the present to write summaries, to describe things and characterise people, to analyse and comment on texts (e. g. literature) and to describe pictures.

> **Tip**
> The **simple present** is often used with the 'signal words' *always, often, regularly, never, sometimes, usually* etc.

> **Tip**
> The **present progressive** is often used with the 'signal words' *at the moment, just now* and *right now*.

Basic rules

Simple present
The **simple present** is used when you express facts or what people accept as true.

You also use the **simple present** when you talk about **things that happen regularly** or **permanent states**.

*The earth **moves** round the sun.*
*A lot of energy **is wasted**.* → Passive, p. 42
*I usually **play** basketball on Mondays.*
*My mother **works** for the local council.*

Present progressive
You use the **present progressive** to describe **activities that are going on at the moment** and **gradual developments**.

*I**'m** just **reading** a very interesting book.*
*It says in the paper today that winters **are getting** milder all the time. Not enough **is being done** to stop global warming.* → Passive, p. 42

1 Activities, habits and facts

Simple present or present progressive? Decide which is most suitable in these short dialogues. → A

a) Sarah: Listen to this! I _____ (read) an article about sleep. It _____ (say) here that people who _____ (sleep) late _____ (live) longer!

Jessica: That _____ (sound) like good news. I must tell my parents! They _____ (always – go) crazy when I _____ (stay) in bed late at the weekends. Sometimes I _____ (not get) up till about one o'clock, and by that time they _____ (start) their lunch! Of course, on the days when we _____ (have) school, I _____ (absolutely – hate) getting up. Sometimes I _____ (not even – hear) the alarm. As you can imagine, Mum _____ (begin) to get fed up – she _____ (often – have to) wake me up!

Sarah: I _____ (know) the problem! But according to the latest research, children and adolescents _____ (do) better at school if they _____ (sleep) till about 8 a.m. The results of tests _____ (prove) beyond doubt that they _____ (concentrate) better and _____ (not get) tired so easily during the day. So now the heads of some schools _____ (actually – discuss) whether to start the school day half an hour later.

Jessica: Great! But I _____ (bet) that won't happen at our school!

Talking about the present

b) Harry: Hi, Mum! I _____ (look) for Dad. Where is he?

Mother: I'm not sure. Perhaps he _____ (work) on that film he _____ (make) of our holiday in Jamaica. Or maybe he _____ (just – watch) TV.

Harry: No, he's not in the house. Maybe he _____ (do) something in the garage.

Mother: It _____ (get) quite late for that, though. Ten o'clock!

Harry: Time for the news on TV! It _____ (just – start) now.

Mother: Right, Harry. Your father is sure to be back in the house in a moment or two. He _____ (never – miss) the ten o'clock news!

B Dynamic verbs and stative verbs

In English, unlike in German, there are two aspects – **simple** and **progressive**.
For each tense (present, past, perfect, future) there is a simple form and a progressive form.
Which of the two aspects you choose often depends on the type of verb you want to use.
All English verbs can be used in the simple form. The progressive form, however, is normally only possible with **verbs that can describe an action in progress.** These verbs are called **dynamic verbs.**

Basic rules

Dynamic verbs

Verbs like *eat, grow, play, rain, read, swim, walk* etc. are **dynamic verbs**. They describe actions and can be used in the **simple** and the **progressive form**. Most verbs belong to this group.

*Our dog always **barks** a lot when visitors **come**.*
*Why's Sammy **barking**? – Someone's **coming** to the front door!*

Stative verbs

Stative verbs are verbs that describe a state and can normally only be used in the **simple form**.
Some of the most common stative verbs are:

- *be, mean, seem, sound, look, cost* – expressing a **state/a quality**
- *have, belong, own* – expressing **possession**
- *know, realise, understand, remember, forget, believe, think, imagine, suppose* – expressing **knowledge/an opinion**
- *want, wish* – expressing **a wish/an intention**
- *like, love, prefer, hate* – expressing **likes/dislikes**
- *notice, see, hear, feel* – expressing **perception**

*London **is** a beautiful city.*
*How much **does** this travel guide **cost**?*
*Buckingham Palace **belongs** to the Royal Family.*
***Do** you **think** it **looks** impressive?*

*I **want** to go to Tate Modern while we're here.*
*Good idea. I **love** art galleries!*
*Oh dear! **Do** you **see** that long queue outside Madame Tussaud's?*

Some of the **stative verbs** above can sometimes also express an activity and can be used in the progressive form. Notice the **difference in meaning**:

simple form (state)	progressive form (activity)
We **have** a holiday cottage down in Cornwall. (… haben …)	We're **having** a great holiday here in Newquay! (… verbringen einen tollen Urlaub …)
Timmy **is** such a happy little boy! (… ist immer guter Laune!)	But he's **being** very difficult today. (… ist/verhält sich …)
The Blue Bay Hotel **looks** quite nice. (… sieht … aus.)	I'm just **looking** at these brochures. (… schaue … an.)
I **think** it's important to enjoy your job. (… glaube/denke …)	Jack **is thinking** of starting his own business. (… überlegt …, ob …)

Talking about the present

2 A question of opinion

*Jokes and anecdotes are often told in the present tense. Cross out the form you think is **wrong** here. (If you are working with a partner, talk about the differences and explain your choice.)* → A, B

Three men (sit / are sitting) together in a pub. While they (have / are having) their last beer, the topic of their conversation (changes / is changing) and they (start / are starting) to talk about moral and religious issues.

"Well," (says / is saying) one of them, "when exactly (does life begin / is life beginning)? What
5 (do you think / are you thinking)?"

The youngest of the three, whose wife (expects / is expecting) a baby, (replies / is replying) without a second thought: "Life (begins / is beginning) on conception, of course!" The second man (disagrees / is disagreeing): "Surely not! I (believe / am believing) life (begins / is beginning) when the baby (is born / is being born)." "Rubbish!" (says / is saying) the third
10 man, the oldest of the three. "My wife and I (have / are having) three children. The eldest (spends / is spending) a year in the States, the middle one (studies / is studying) medicine, and the youngest (just starts / is just starting) university. And I can tell you: life (doesn't really start / isn't really starting) till the children (leave / are leaving) home and the dog (dies / is dying)!"

7 conception *Empfängnis*

3 Activities and states

> **Tip**
>
> The adverb *always* is normally a signal word for the **simple form**. But it can also be used with the **progressive form**. In that case it describes the speaker's annoyance or irritation.

Rephrase these sentences, using the verbs in brackets, and deciding whether to use the simple or the progressive form. (Sometimes you will need 'always'.) → B

Examples: My father often reads the paper *at breakfast*. (have)
 – My father often reads the paper while he is having breakfast.
 My mother never stops *criticising* my friends. (criticise) ☹
 – My mother is always criticising my friends.

1. Maybe *I'll buy* a new laptop. (think of) _____
2. These *aren't my* CDs. (belong) _____
3. When *is your usual breakfast time*? (have) _____
_____
4. *In my opinion*, we ought to change our plans. (feel) _____
5. How much *is* this T-shirt, please? (cost) _____
6. Jim *keeps leaving* his clothes on the floor – I *hate that*! (leave) ☹ _____
_____
7. You're *behaving* in a very silly way! (be) _____
8. Your *money goes* on such useless things. *How foolish*! (spend) ☹ _____
_____
9. *I like* Jennifer's new dress. *It's* very attractive. (think; look) _____
_____
10. *Our* holiday here in Wales *is* great! (have) _____
11. I *keep losing* my keys. *How stupid I am!* (lose) ☹ _____
12. *Is* this *your uncle's* restaurant? (own) _____
13. We never watch TV *at lunch*. (have) _____
14. *I've no idea* what you're talking about. (know) _____

Talking about the present

4 Asking questions in the present tense

Complete the short dialogues with appropriate questions. → A, B

1. – My grandparents are French.
   – Really? _____?
   – No, in Switzerland, actually. They've got a house near Geneva.

2. – It's a beautiful castle, isn't it?
   – It certainly is! Who_____?
   – I'm not quite sure, but I think it may belong to the Fitzgerald family.

3. – We can't always take our dog with us when we go on holiday.
   – Who _____ then?
   – My aunt usually does.

4. – My uncle used to be in the army. Now he writes history books.
   – How interesting! _____ at the moment?
   – Yes! He's in the middle of one. It's going to be about the Gulf war.

5. – My parents are both teachers.
   – _____ at the same school?
   – Oh no! My dad works at the local comprehensive, and my mum's a primary school teacher.

5 What's the difference here?

Simple and progressive forms are often used without signal words. Explain the differences in meaning between these sentence pairs. → A

Example: My uncle sleeps in that room. (It's his bedroom.)
– My uncle is sleeping in that room. (Don't go in there! He's asleep.)

1. Jack plays golf. (_____)
   Jack is playing golf. (_____)
2. Dad isn't watching TV. (_____)
   Dad doesn't watch TV. (_____)
3. Kim is practising the flute in the guest room. (_____)
   Kim practises the flute in the guest room. (_____)
4. Does your mother work? (_____)
   Is your mother working? (_____)

6 Well-known proverbs

Complete these proverbs with the verbs below. Then choose three of them, and explain their meaning. → A

stand • shut • live • fall • stink • come • open • speak • make

Example: "Silence means consent." This means that if you don't give your opinion on something, for example someone else's suggestion, people assume you agree with it.

1. Nothing _____ of nothing.
2. When one door _____ , another one _____ .
3. Those who _____ in glass houses shouldn't throw stones.
4. Fish and guests _____ after three days.
5. Practice _____ perfect.
6. Actions _____ louder than words.
7. United we _____, divided we _____.

Talking about the present

7 A cartoon

What might the other hamster reply? → A, B
Think of 4 – 5 answers, using the present (simple or progressive). These ideas may help you:

want	try
enjoy	train for
feel	think

"Don't you think you're taking this exercise wheel a bit too seriously?"

C The present tense sequence

The relationship between the different tenses in a text is called the **sequence of tenses**.

> ### Basic rules
>
> **Sequence of tenses and summary writing**
>
> When the **present** tense is the basic tense, it is generally used together with the **present perfect**, the **past tense** and the ***will* future**.
> The basic tense of summaries is the **present tense**.
>
> Compare how the other tenses in this summary are connected to it.
>
> | | |
> | --- | --- |
> | This is the introduction to the summary. It refers to the time when the text was written, in the past. | *William Shakespeare probably **wrote** 'Romeo and Juliet' in 1595. It **was** first **performed** in the same year and **appeared** in print in 1597.* |
> | This is the basic tense. It describes actions and events. | *The play **starts** with a violent quarrel between the servants of the Capulets and the Montagues in the streets of Verona.* |
> | The **present perfect progressive** describes actions or events that started in the past and are still going on. | *The two families **have been fighting** each other for generations.*

 *The Prince **appears** and **stops** the fight.* |
> | The **present perfect simple** describes the result of past events.

 The ***will* future** refers to future events. | *The continuous disturbances of the peace in Verona **have enraged** him, and he **declares** that "whoever **disturbs** the peace of our streets again" **will pay** for this with their lives.*

 *A few days later Capulet **plans** a masked ball for his daughter Juliet.* |
> | The **present perfect simple** describes a state that started in the past and is still relevant. | *Romeo, the son of Montague, decides to go to this ball because he **expects** that he will find Rosaline there, whom he **has been** desperately in love with for some time.* |
> | The **simple present** also describes a series of actions and events. | *At the ball he and Juliet **meet** and immediately **fall** in love. After the ball Romeo **waits** under Juliet's balcony, and they **arrange** a secret marriage. The marriage **takes place** and **is** immediately **followed** by disaster, when …* |

Talking about the present

8 Not so beautiful after all?

Complete the text with verb forms that belong to the present tense sequence. Sometimes more than one form may be possible. → C

Everyone _____ (know) how fashion magazines and TV _____ (give) teenage girls the impression that they _____ (need) to be thin if they _____ (want) to look beautiful. It's a problem that parents – and doctors – _____ (worry) about for years. But now, psychologists at the University of Texas _____ (discover) a new way of counteracting the problem, which they _____ (call) the Body Project.

Over the last few years, over a thousand American high school and college students _____ (take) part in the Body Project. Here's the way it _____ (work). First of all, girls _____ (be taught) to realise how they _____ (be tricked) by the fashion magazines into thinking that only thin people _____ (have) a chance of true happiness or success in their lives. After they _____ (learn) to criticise the 'thin ideal' through essay-writing and role-play exercises, they _____ (be encouraged) to 'protest' in public. So far, some girls _____ (write) letters to the makers of the 'Barbie' doll, for example, while others _____ (go) into book shops, putting little notes saying "Your body is beautiful already! You don't have to be thin" between the pages of books about slimming.

When they _____ (complete) the project, most of the girls _____ (feel) much more positive about their bodies.

"Before the programme," one of the girls _____ (report), "I used to think: If I _____ (not be) really thin, nobody _____ (find) me attractive. But now I _____ (realise) it's all a trick. These people in the fashion industry _____ (want) you to feel unsure of yourself, so that you _____ (buy) the things they _____ (advertise), and as a result, of course, they _____ (make) money. But now, thanks to all the exercises and stuff we _____ (do) all these weeks, I _____ (manage) to put all those stupid ideas behind me! I _____ (not fall) into that trap again! Never!"

Talking about the present

9 The Break In

This is an extract from We Are All Guilty, *a short novel by Kingsley Amis. Clive Rayner, 17, is frustrated and bored. He is out of work, bullied by his stepfather and criticised by his mother. One evening, when he is out with his friend Terry, he suddenly thinks of a way to bring some 'excitement' into life …*

Read the text carefully, then write a summary. To prepare, mark the parts of the text that seem most important. Keep to the present tense sequence. Avoid direct speech. You may find some of these verbs useful to start you off: suggest, understand, explain, persuade, fear, doubt, convince → C

"You know Butterfield Brothers?"

"Yeah. Warehouse place, ennit. Just round the corner from here."

"You and me, we're going to do it."

5 "What? Why, what's there? What are you talking about?"

"Electrical … apparatus," said Clive. "And that kind of thing."

"How do you mean?"

10 "Toasters are electrical. And fires. I don't know. Lots of stuff. We'll see what there is when we get in there."

"What, you mean break in and pinch stuff?"

15 "Got it, mastermind. Let's get going, we're wasting time."

"But there'll be dogs and guards," said Terry, still blinking in surprise and shock, but getting on his feet. "You know, Securicor. You know, blokes with helmets and sticks."

"Not there, it's all run down. And they always have a notice saying about dogs and guards
20 if there's any there, or even if there isn't, and they don't have one there. We can get over that gate in half a minute flat."

Clive turned out to be right about the gate of Butterfield Bros., and he and Terry soon had a window broken, in fact it was cracked already so it was more just pushing it in, and soon they were inside the place with no trouble at all. They looked round. There was not much to
25 see, apart from damp-stains, empty metal containers and a steep narrow staircase leading to a narrow catwalk with a guard-rail along it. Clive led the way up the stairs and they had just reached the catwalk when a bell started ringing some distance off.

Terry pulled at the back of Clive's bomber jacket. "Come on, let's get out of here," he said in a loud whisper.

30 "Shut up and listen. I don't think there's anyone around."

The bell stopped and silence followed. Half a minute. More.

"Right, move it," said Clive. "Just automatic, that thing."

He turned a corner, still on the catwalk, and straight away a man came out of an opening in the wall and started running towards him and shouting, a stocky middle-aged man with
35 a clipped moustache. He looked and sounded quite fierce and this catwalk thing, ten or fifteen feet from the floor, was no place to start an argument. In no time at all Clive and Terry were running back the way they had come as fast as they could, which was not very fast with so little room to spare.

Terry got to the top of the staircase, then Clive, who had noticed that just there the guard-
40 rail had broken away and been roughly repaired with wood and wire. And it was just there that the man chasing them caught the collar of Clive's jacket. They struggled for a moment, Clive only trying to get free, not hitting the man or even pushing him, but unintentionally throwing him off balance. The man's foot slipped on the metal and he grabbed at the weak part of the rail. It gave way and he cried out and fell, landing below with a thump that Clive
45 never forgot.

But for now he thought only of getting away. He clattered down the stairs at top speed, saw an outside door, ran to it and started shifting bolts. He shouted to Terry to come on, and Terry shouted back something about the bloke being hurt. Clive wasted no more time, but got the door open and ran out.

From: Kingsley Amis, *We Are All Guilty*, 1991.

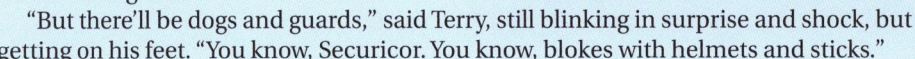

2 **warehouse** ['weəhaʊs] *Lagerhalle, Lager* • 13 **to pinch** to steal • 19 **run down** *baufällig, heruntergekommen* • 26 **catwalk** *Arbeitsbrücke, -steg* • 26 **guard-rail** *Geländer* • 44 **thump** a dull heavy, sound • 47 **to shift** to move • 47 **bolt** [bəʊlt] *Riegel*

Talking about the present

10 Error spotting

Read this text on 'Animal Farm', written by a student. Some of the verb forms have been marked. Decide if they are right or wrong and write down the corrected forms where necessary. → C

Animal Farm, which has been written (1) by George Orwell and first published in 1945, is taking (2) the form of a fable. It is a political satire on dictatorship in general, and the condition and situation of the animals on the farm are representing (3) the lives of the Russian people during and after the Russian Revolution.

The story begins (4) when Old Major, the prize boar on the farm, is inspiring (5) all the animals to revolt against their human master, Mr Jones, who had been treating (6) them all very badly for years. Old Major explains (7) that if they are managing (8) to drive Mr Jones and his men out, they are able to (9) look after the farm themselves in the future. Soon afterwards, their revolution succeeded (10), and the pigs become (11) the new leaders.

After Mr Jones had been driven (12) out, life on the farm is still hard, but the animals, inspired by their motto 'All animals are equal', are happy at first, especially when they are remembering (13) the old days when Mr Jones was owning (14) the farm. Eventually, however, the pigs, dominated by their leader, Napoleon, were corrupted (15) by power, and a new tyranny is replacing (16) the old. Even their beloved motto is changed (17) by the régime to 'All animals are equal but some animals are more equal than others'. Napoleon, the brutal leader of the pigs, is standing (18) for Stalin, whereas Boxer, the hard-working carthorse who is ruthlessly driven off to the knacker's when his strength finally fails (19), is a tragic figure who represented (20) the good nature of the ordinary people under a totalitarian system.

1. _____
2. _____
3. _____
4. _____
5. _____
6. _____
7. _____
8. _____
9. _____
10. _____
11. _____
12. _____
13. _____
14. _____
15. _____
16. _____
17. _____
18. _____
19. _____
20. _____

5 **boar** male pig • 17 **carthorse** a large, strong horse used for pulling heavy loads • 17 **knacker's** Abdecker

11 Mediation: Kampf gegen die bunte Beutelpest

Read this German newspaper article, marking the facts you find most important. Then write a summary in English, using the present tense sequence. You may need a dictionary. → C

Milliarden weggeworfener Plastiktüten flattern um den Globus

Australien will sie jetzt verbieten. Sie sind praktisch, bunt, wasserdicht, reißfest und kosten fast nichts. Sie sind weltweit unterwegs, nach Gebrauch hängen sie in Sträuchern und Zäunen, schwimmen im Meer oder wirbeln durch die Luft. Jetzt soll es ihnen an die Tragegriffe gehen: Der australische Umweltminister Peter Garrett will Plastiktüten verbieten lassen. „Es fliegen schätzungsweise vier Milliarden Tüten herum, landen auf Müllkippen, bedrohen unsere Wildtiere und verschmutzen unsere Strände," sagt Garrett. Vier Milliarden nur in Australien, rund um den Globus sind es weit mehr, allein in den USA werden pro Jahr 86 Milliarden der Kunststoffbeutel verbraucht.

Kritik an den Plänen Garretts kam vom Vorsitzenden des australischen Einzelhandelsverband, Richard Evans: „Papiertüten sind auch nicht umweltfreundlicher, Plastiktüten gehören zu unserem Leben." Dazu gehören sie tatsächlich, und das noch sehr lange. Die Umweltbehörde der Vereinten Nationen (Unep) schätzt, dass Plastiktüten zwischen 400 und 1000 Jahren brauchen, bis sie komplett verfallen sind. Dabei sind die Tüten nur die gut sichtbare Spitze des Plastikmüllberges, der immer höher wird. Wegen des langsamen Verfalls ist das meiste des seit den frühen 50er Jahren des vergangenen Jahrhunderts verstärkt hergestellten Plastiks noch da. Und es steckt überall. In Küchengeräten, Autos, Zahnbürsten und, in der Landschaft besonders auffällig, in Tüten. In vielen Ländern hat sich um Dörfer und Städte ein Ring von Plastiktüten gelegt, die dann lange die Landschaft verschandeln. Auch in Australien ist das ein Problem. „Abfalltechnisch leben die Australier noch im letzten Jahrhundert," sagt Professor Klaus Wiemer, Leiter des Fachgebiets Abfallwirtschaft und Altlasten an der Uni Kassel. Zwischen Sydney und Perth landet der Müll meist auf Deponien, von dort fliegen die Tüten dann ins Outback, landen an der Küste oder im Meer.

Südwest Presse, 17. 1. 2008

Talking about the past

A The past tense

There are three basic tenses in English that refer to the past: **past tense**, **present perfect** and **past perfect**. Each of them has a **simple** and a **progressive form**.

The **past tense** is generally used
- when people talk about things that happened in the past or when you write stories or letters that refer to the past
- in novels, short stories and reports.

> **Tip**
> The **simple past** is often used with adverbials of past time (*last year, in 1999, 400 years ago, yesterday*, etc.), and in questions with *when* (*When **did** you **see** the play?*)

Basic rules

Simple past

You use the **simple past** to describe past states, events or activities that were completed in the past and are now over. They are not directly relevant to the present.

*When we **were** in London <u>last year</u>, we **looked** at the Globe theatre.*
***Did** you **see** a performance there?*
*No, we **weren't able** to get tickets, so we **didn't see** a play.*
*The new Globe **was finished** <u>in 1997</u>.*
*It **was built** near the place where Shakespeare's Globe **stood** <u>400 years ago</u>.*

The **simple past** is also used to describe a series of actions or events. This makes it the basic tense in narrative texts (stories, novels) and reports about past events.

*As soon as he **heard** the noise, Harry **got up** from his chair. He **switched off** the lights and **went** to the front door. He **opened** it slowly. It **was** dark outside and he **couldn't** see a thing. Then, suddenly, ...*

Past progressive

> **Tip**
> The **past progressive** often appears in clauses with *while* and the **simple past** in clauses with *when*.

The **past progressive** describes activities that were in progress at a certain time in the past. It is used in scenic descriptions.
The **past progressive** is often used to describe something that was still going on when something new happened. In this case the **past progressive** is used for the background activity and the simple past for the new event.

*Amy and I **were** just **coming** out of the Underground <u>when</u> a thunderstorm started.*
*<u>While</u> we **were waiting** for it to stop, we saw an enormous flash of lightning.*
*We **were having** tea in a café <u>when</u> all the lights suddenly went out.*

The **past progressive** is also used to describe several activities that were going on at the same time in the past, and for gradual developments.

*It was still quite early, but lots of people **were** already **lying** on the beach, and a few **were** even **swimming**. The sun **was shining** brightly and it **was beginning** to get really hot.*

> **Tip**
> When you have written a text in the **past tense**, just check again and make sure that you have got the correct **simple past** forms of the irregular verbs.

1 Checking your past tense forms

Fill in the past tense forms of these verbs: → A

1. to prefer: _____
2. to die: _____
3. to develop: _____
4. to flow: _____
5. to let: _____
6. to cry: _____
7. to shake: _____
8. to flee: _____
9. to sink: _____
10. to throw: _____
11. to hear: _____
12. to fly: _____
13. to lay: _____
14. to swim: _____
15. to bear: _____
16. to lend: _____
17. to brake: _____
18. to feed: _____
19. to begin: _____
20. to overtake: _____

Talking about the past

2 A helpful orang-utan

*To complete this letter to the editor of a newspaper, you will need to use **past tense** forms. Decide when to use the simple past – and when to use the past progressive. Sometimes both forms may be suitable.* → A

It _____ (happen) while I _____ (visit) the orang-utan sanctuary at Camp Leakey in Borneo some years ago. Early on the first morning, while it _____ (be) still dark, I _____ (go) out and _____ (start) to walk in the direction of the river. At the side of the path I _____ (just – be able to) make out a large orang-utan with a smaller one that _____ (sit) on her lap. As she _____ (look) so friendly, I _____ (stop) and _____ (speak) to her. In response she _____ (take) my hand in a friendly way. I _____ (stand) there for a while, talking to her, but when I _____ (want) to leave, I _____ (find) that she _____ (hold) my hand so tightly that I _____ (not be able to) move. Time _____ (pass) and after a while, just as the sky _____ (begin) to get lighter, she suddenly _____ (let) my hand go. I _____ (say) goodbye and _____ (walk) on, but as I _____ (approach) the river, I _____ (notice) that a large crocodile _____ (lie) on the path about 50 yards ahead of me, and that it _____ (look) at me speculatively. We _____ (stare) at each other for what _____ (seem) an eternity; then it _____ (move) off and into the river, with a huge splash. I _____ (walk) back quickly, and when I _____ (tell) one of the Dayak guides my story, he _____ (laugh). Apparently the orang-utan – he _____ (call) her Princess – _____ (come) to the sanctuary every day for her breakfast. She _____ (know) that that crocodile _____ (be) there, but she _____ (also – know) that crocodiles _____ (attack) only at night. By holding me back until she _____ (judge) that the sky _____ (get) light enough, she had saved me from being eaten for breakfast! I _____ (feel) so thankful that I _____ (take) Princess a big bunch of bananas.

1 **sanctuary** Schutzgebiet • 2 **lap** Schoß

Talking about the past

3 What's the difference?

Sometimes the choice between the past progressive and the simple past can affect the meaning of a sentence. Compare the two: → A

a) Everybody **was laughing** when we came into the room. (*Meaning:* People had started laughing about something before we came in.)
b) Everybody **laughed** when we came into the room. (*Meaning:* People started laughing – at us, probably! – when they saw us come in.)

Now put in the form that you think is suitable in each of these sentences. Then explain your choice. The decision is between: 1. One thing happened immediately after the other or was even caused by it, and 2. Something was already in progress – in the background – when another thing happened.

1. When she switched the light on, I _____ (wake up).
   (*Meaning:* _____)
2. The dog _____ (bark) when the door bell rang.
   (*Meaning:* _____)
3. I couldn't answer the phone because I _____ (have) a shower.
   (*Meaning:* _____)
4. Can you remember where you were and what you _____ (do) when you heard the news of the terrorist attack? (*Meaning:* _____)
5. When he got back to his seat after the interval, someone else _____ (sit) in his place. (*Meaning:* _____)
6. Who _____ (fetch) the doctor when Uncle Ted fell off the ladder in the orchard? (*Meaning:* _____)

B The present perfect

The **present perfect** connects the past to the present.

Tip	Basic rules
The **present perfect simple** is often used with *already, just, (not) yet, ever, never, so far, for and since*, and with expressions of frequency (*twice*).	**Present perfect simple** The **present perfect simple** is used when you want to stress the result of an activity. The time at which the activity occurred is not relevant. The activity itself happened in the past, but the result is still relevant in the present. *I've read that novel already.* → *So you don't need to lend it to me.* *A new film has just been made of the book.* → *Let's watch it.* *Jim has lost his car keys.* → *Now he has to walk home.*
Tip For English sentences with **for** and **since** you can often use the *Präsens + schon* in German (*Der Pub gehört der Familie schon seit …*).	It can also be used to express that something hasn't happened yet or to ask whether something has taken place yet: With **stative verbs** (→ p. 5) the **present perfect simple** can express that a state began in the past and still continues in the present.	*She hasn't had the chance to go to Britain yet.* *Have you ever been to the United States? – Yes, I've been to New York twice.* *We've known the Wilsons for a long time.* *The pub has belonged to the family since the 18th century.*
Tip The **present perfect progressive** is often used with **for** and **since**. **For** is used for a period of time (*for ages*). **Since** is used for a point in time (*since 7 o'clock*)	**Present perfect progressive** The **present perfect progressive** is normally only used with dynamic verbs (→ p. 5) It describes an activity that began in the past and has continued until now (and may still continue). It stresses the duration and continuation of an activity.	*I'm dead tired. We've been looking round the shops for hours!* *You've been complaining ever since we left home this morning.*

Talking about the past

4 Relationships

a) *Fill in the correct verb forms: past tense or present perfect, simple or progressive.* → A, B

1. When I _____ (see) Julie yesterday, I _____ (think) she _____ (not look) very happy. – No, you're right, she's devastated. _____ (you – not hear) yet? Her boyfriend _____ (just – dump) her.

2. How long _____ (you know) Clive? – Ever since we _____ (be) at nursery school together! – Well, _____ (you – ever – think) he might be in love with you? – Of course not! – Well, open your eyes, Sally! He _____ (look) at you non-stop for weeks in a very special way, and you _____ (not even – notice)!

3. When _____ (you – meet) Jessica? – About three months ago. It _____ (be) in the summer. I _____ (be) on the beach, and she _____ (sit) nearby with a friend. I _____ (think) how attractive she _____ (look), so I _____ (ask) her the time, and that's how we _____ (get) into conversation. When the two of them _____ (get) ready to leave, I _____ (offer) them a lift home in my car. – So that's how it all _____ (start), then! – Yes, Jessica and I _____ (go) out together ever since. She's the nicest girlfriend I _____ (ever – have).

4. What a lovely wedding photo! – Yes, it's my parents. They're still very happy. They _____ (be) married for nearly 25 years, and my mum says they _____ (never – have) a quarrel. – I don't believe it! My mum says her wedding day _____ (be) the happiest day of her life, but as far as I can see, things _____ (change) quite a bit since then!

b) *Explain the use of tenses in the cartoon.* → A, B

c) *Imagine the two women go on talking about their weddings and their husbands. Continue their dialogue, using the past tense and the present perfect wherever you can.* → A, B

"No, I didn't cry on my wedding day. I have done every day since though."

Talking about the past

5 The joys of surfing in the UK

Past tense or present perfect? Simple or progressive? Use the 'bits and pieces' to make sentences with suitable verb forms. → A, B

1. "you – ever – do – any surfing?" – "yes – go – surfing – Cornwall – last summer!"
   _____
   _____

2. 50 years ago – surfing – be – sport that – be known – chiefly – Hawaii, California or Australia.
   _____
   _____

3. but – recently – it – become – very popular – UK. _____
   _____

4. in the 1960s – the first Australians – arrive – Newquay – and – begin – work as lifeguards.
   _____
   _____

5. they – teach – local boys (like Roger Mansfield – who – become – British champion – 1970) – the art of surfing. _____
   _____
   _____

6. *Roger:* "1963 – if – you – go – beach in Newquay – perhaps – 10 to 15 people – surf. Now – best beaches – get – terribly crowded! Newquay – change – completely!"
   _____
   _____
   _____

7. Chris Jones – make – surfboards – Newquay – since 1965. _____
   _____

8. *Chris:* "the sport – become – more accessible – over the past 20 years or so – because – wet-suits – improve – so much. Surfing – Cornwall – develop – into – all-year-round sport!"
   _____
   _____
   _____
   _____

6 What's that in English?

Past tense or present perfect? Put these simple 'everyday' sentences into English. → A, B

1. "Wann hast du Julia das letzte Mal gesehen?" – "Ich habe sie in letzter Zeit überhaupt nicht gesehen." _____
   _____

2. „Ich hab' den Kuchen gestern abend gebacken." _____

3. „Wir warten schon ewig auf dich! Was hast du denn die ganze Zeit gemacht?"
   _____
   _____

4. „Ich saß gerade im Garten, als du angerufen hast." _____
   _____

Talking about the past

7 Drought in Australia

I love a sunburnt country,
A land of sweeping plains,
Of ragged mountain ranges,
Of droughts and flooding rains.
I love her far horizons,
I love her jewel-sea,
Her beauty and her terror –
The wide brown land for me!

From: My Country by Dorothea MacKellar

First read the text. As you go, mark the past tense and present perfect forms (in different colours) in the text. → A, B

The poet Dorothea MacKellar once wrote these well-known lines about her beloved Australia: "I love a sunburnt country, a land of sweeping plains." That was back in 1904. But the land MacKellar loved is now cracked and dangerously dry, and the two rivers that gave the Murray-Darling basin its name have been reduced to slow-flowing brown streams.
5 Australia, the world's driest continent, is in the grip of the worst drought in its recorded history.
   The long period of dry weather, which began in 2002, has affected the Murray-Darling basin particularly badly. For farmers, many of whom have been growing crops in the region for decades, the situation is desperate. Those with cattle and sheep stations are no better off.
10 With paddocks that have turned into dust bowls, many farmers have been forced to sell off their animals at rock-bottom prices. Some have already given up, leaving behind sheep and cattle stations that have been in their families for generations. In this baking hot land, the suicide rate has rocketed, and in rural areas is now 20 % higher than in the cities.
   In September 2007, with no prospect of rain and no chance of government-controlled
15 water, some farmers were unable to plant any grain. This meant that in May 2008, at a time when farmers would normally have been bringing in their harvest, some had nothing to bring in at all. Especially crops such as rice, cotton and wine grapes have failed, and citrus, almond and olive trees have died. In a normal year, about 1.2 million metric tons of rice are produced by Australia's 2000 rice farmers. In 2008 the harvest was only 18,000 tons. Some
20 farmers have turned to wheat as a less 'thirsty' alternative, although drought halved wheat production in 2002–3.
   The causes of the drought are complex. But most scientists agree that global warming has played a part. Average temperatures in Australia, which have risen by 0.7° over the last 100 years, are expected to go up by anything between 1° and 6° over the next 60 years.

Now answer these questions on the text to show you have understood it. Use past tense and present perfect forms appropriately. → A, B

1. What is the problem affecting the Murray-Darling basin? When did it start, and what effects has it had on farmers there? (Refer to lines 1–13.) _____
   _____
   _____
   _____

2. What happened as a result of the dry weather in September 2007? _____
   _____
   _____

3. What seems to be one of the reasons for the long drought? _____
   _____

4. Who was Dorothea MacKellar and what is she famous for? _____
   _____

Talking about the past

C Related tenses

The **past perfect** is the tense that goes back furthest into the past.

Basic rules

Past perfect simple

The **past perfect** describes what happened before another activity or event in the past. The **past perfect** is nearly always used together with past tense forms. In this case the **past tense** describes what happened at a certain time in the past (*then, at that time*) and the **past perfect** states what happened *before that time*.

*After we **had checked** in at our hotel, we all went straight down to the beach.*
*Alice was delighted to find that she**'d been given** a room with a sea view.*
*Before we left home, I**'d made** a list of all the places I wanted to see.*
*None of us **had** ever **been** to Greece before.*

Past perfect progressive

The **past perfect progressive** expresses that an activity was in progress before another activity in the past.

*She **had been looking** forward to seeing the film ever since she had heard about it.*
*But she**'d** only **been watching** it for a few minutes when she realized how stupid it was.*

Other tenses

When the past tense is the basic tense, both **was/were going to** and the **conditional** are used to refer to the future.
The **conditional** often appears in indirect speech.

*He **was going to** practise more, but he knew that he **would** never **be** quite as good at tennis as Mike.*

The **conditional perfect** is used in conditional sentences which refer to the past.

*Perhaps he **would have won** their last match if he hadn't injured his leg in the second set.*

The construction **auxiliary + perfect infinitive** of a main verb can also refer to the past.

*Our neighbours **must have seen** the burglars.*
*They **should have called** the police.*
*The burglars **could** easily **have been arrested**.*

This construction often corresponds to a subjunctive construction in German.

*Unsere Nachbarn **hätten** die Polizei **rufen sollen**.*
*Die Einbrecher **hätten** ganz einfach **verhaftet werden können**.*

Tip
Sentences in the **past perfect** often contain *after*, *before* and *when*. Like the present perfect, the **past perfect** is also often used with *ever* or *never*.

Tip
Like the **present perfect progressive**, the **past perfect progessive** is often used with *for* and *since*.

Tip
Would + infinitive can also express a habitual activity in the past.
*When my grandfather was a small boy he and his friends **would** often **play** football in the street.*
You often find this use of *would* in narrative texts (see exercise 13).

8 Using related tenses

Choose the correct verb form. Underline the correct form, or cross out the one that is wrong.
→ A, B, C

1. When I (was getting/got) home last night, I (have discovered/discovered) that I (had forgotten/have forgotten) my keys.

2. Mike (has failed/failed) his driving test last week. He (had passed/would have passed) if he (didn't drive/hadn't driven) over a crossing when the traffic lights (would have been/were) red.

3. When we (saw/had seen) Amy yesterday, we (have told/told) her about our party, but unfortunately she (had said/said) she (wouldn't be able to/hadn't been able to) come.

4. My grandparents (moved/have moved) into a new flat last month. They (had looked/had been looking) for a suitable place for ages. At one point they (had thought/had been thinking) they (will never find/would never find) anything they really (liked/had liked).

5. You (needn't have helped/needn't help) Sam yesterday. He (had easily done/could easily have done) everything on his own.

6. John (felt/had felt) very disappointed when he (was discovering/discovered) that the job he (would apply for/was going to apply for) (was given/had been given) to someone else.

Talking about the past

D The past tense sequence

The sequence of tenses is the relationship between tenses and depends on the basic tense in a text. In Chapter 1 the present tense sequence was introduced. There is also a **past tense sequence**.

Basic rules

Past tense sequence

When the **past tense** is the basic tense in a text, it is generally used together with the **past perfect** and the **conditional** or **conditional perfect**.

- The **past perfect** is used to refer to a point or period in time further back in the past.
- The **conditional** or *was/were going to* are used to refer to the future,
- The **conditional perfect** is used for theoretical conditions referring to the past.

9 The dead duck

In this excerpt from About a boy *Marcus, a twelve-year old boy, has gone to Regent's Park together with his mother's friend Suzie, her baby Megan, and Will, who is "trying to get off with Suzie." Marcus has been throwing bread at the ducks in the pond and has accidentally killed one of them.*

Tip

The **conditional** (*would* + **infinitive**) is sometimes referred to as '**the future in the past**'.

a) Read the text and the annotations for the marked verb forms explaining what the tenses are called and why they are used. → D

Marcus **couldn't believe**[1] it. Dead. A dead duck. OK, he'**d been trying**[2] to hit it on the head with a piece of sandwich, but he tried to do all sorts of things, and none of them **had** ever **happened**[3] before. He'd tried to get the highest score on the Stargazer
5 machine in the kebab shop on Hornsey Road – nothing. It really annoyed him that the only thing he'd ever achieved through trying was something he hadn't really wanted to do that much in the first place. And anyway, since when did hitting a bird with a sandwich ever kill it? Kids must spend half their lives throwing things at the
10 ducks in Regent's Park. How come he managed to pick a duck that pathetic? There **must have been**[4] something wrong with it. It was probably just about to die from a heart attack or something; it was just a coincidence. But if it **was**, nobody **would believe**[5] him. If there **were** any witnesses, they'**d** only **have seen**[6] the bread
15 hit the duck right on the back of the head, and then seen it keel over. They'**d put**[7] two and two together and make five, and he'd be imprisoned for a crime he never committed.
    Will, Suzie, Megan and Marcus stood on the path at the edge of the lake, staring at the dead body floating in the water.
20 "There's nothing we can do about it now," said Will, the trendy bloke who **was trying**[8] to get off with Suzie. "Just leave it. What's the problem?"

From: Nick Hornby, *About a boy*, 1998

1 **Past:** This is the basic narrative tense.
2 **Past perfect progressive:** This describes what was in progress before.
3 **Past perfect simple:** This describes what happened or didn't happen before.
4 **Must + perfect infinitive:** It refers to the past and expresses that something seems logical or obvious.
5 **Conditional sentence (past/conditional):** It describes a logical consequence seen from the past.
6 **Conditional sentence (past/conditional perfect):** It expresses a theoretical condition.
7 **Conditional:** This expresses a future possibility seen from the past.
8 **Past progressive:** It describes an activity that was in progress in the past

b) Complete the sentences to show that you have understood the text, using the past tense sequence. Do not quote word for word from the text. → D

1. The duck died after Marcus _____

2. He often tried to do things, but so far _____

3. He feared that even if the duck's death had been a coincidence, people _____

4. In fact he even feared he _____

Talking about the past

10 The Nobel Prize

Complete the anecdote with suitable verb forms. Keep to the past tense sequence. Sometimes more than one form may be possible. → D

A few years ago, an American scientist, who _____ (be awarded) the Nobel Prize in Physics, _____ (give) his acceptance speech in Stockholm.

He _____ (tell) the audience that only a few weeks earlier, he and his wife _____ (drive) through the Arizona desert in their car. "After a while," he _____ (say), "we _____ (come) to a very old-looking gas station in the middle of the desert and _____ (stop) for gas."

"The attendant _____ (come) over to give us a hand – a thin, dirty-looking man who _____ (wear) faded blue overalls and shoes that _____ (fall) apart. As soon as my wife _____ (set) eyes on this man, to my great surprise, she _____ (jump) out of the car, _____ (run) up to him with open arms and _____ (hug) him.

"While they _____ (kiss) passionately, I _____ (go) round to the pump and _____ (fill) up the car myself. Frankly, I _____ (feel) too amazed to speak!

"When we _____ (eventually – drive) off, I _____ (ask) my wife, who _____ (still – blow) kisses to the man we _____ (leave) behind, for an explanation. She _____ (tell) me that she _____ (know) the man years ago when they _____ (be) at college together. In fact, at one point, they _____ (plan) to get married.

"'Hm! Your life _____ (be) a lot different if you _____ (marry) him,' I _____ (say) to her."

"'Oh, I'm not so sure about that,' she _____ (reply) . 'If I _____ (marry) him, maybe *he* _____ (win) the Nobel Prize.'"

11 A 21st century "Miss Marple"

Read this article and mark the parts you find most important. Then write a slightly shorter version of the text in English, keeping to the past tense sequence. (Don't try to translate the article. Just explain what happened. The words in the box will help you.) → D

orphan • doormat
• care home •
handwriting •
workman • to swindle

„Miss Marple" fängt Mörder

LONDON Eine echte „Miss Marple" wie die betagte Detektivin in Agatha Christies Romanen hat in England im Alleingang einen Mörder enttarnt. Dafür bekam die 82-jährige Audrey Ridpath 25,000 Pfund Belohnung. Den Großteil davon will sie Waisenkindern in Ruanda spenden, „damit aus diesem Übel zumindest noch etwas Gutes erwachsen kann".

Der kriminalistische Spürsinn der Witwe aus dem Küstenort Worthing war gefragt, als die 87-jährige Jean Barnes eines Tages ermordet aufgefunden wurde. Ein Einbrecher hatte die Alleinstehende erschlagen. Damit die Tat möglichst lange unbemerkt blieb, hatte er für den Milchmann einen Zettel auf die Fußmatte gelegt, dass Mrs Barnes in ein Pflegeheim gekommen sei. Die Polizei kam in dem Fall nicht weiter. Deshalb zeigte sie in einer britischen TV-Sendung über ungelöste Kriminalfälle den Zettel. Mrs Ridpath sah die Sendung und erkannte die Schrift: 1997 hatte der Handwerker David Munley (57) versucht, eine ihrer Nachbarinnen zu betrügen. Die aufmerksame Ridpath hatte jedoch seine Absichten erkannt und die Frau rechtzeitig gewarnt. Sofort nach der Sendung rief sie die Polizei an und schlug einen Schriftvergleich vor. Das Ergebnis verriet Munley als Mörder.

„Seitdem nennen mich alle nur noch Miss Marple", sagte die grauhaarige Dame. „Ich bin das jetzt eigentlich ein bisschen leid."

dpa (aus *Südwest Presse*, 15.03.2001)

Talking about the past

12 According to plan

Read the opening paragraphs of the short detective story According to plan, *by Ray Darby, noticing the use of the past tense sequence in the narrative.* → D

> It was after nine o'clock when Ben Wayne's taxi drew up at the corner, half a block from Doctor Ridgeway's white house in suburban Lynwood. Ben paid the driver, being careful to keep his face averted and the hat pulled low over his eyes. He mentally cursed that hat. It was quite a trick to keep it on his head at all, because it was at least two sizes too small.
>
> 5   As the taxi pulled away, Ben straightened his tie and smoothed the jacket of the double-breasted suit he had taken off the man in the jail corridor. The suit fitted him better than the hat, although Ben hated gray. He had always been a smart dresser, preferring browns or the darker tweeds. He hoped the guy in the corridor was still unconscious. If he came to and worked the gag off, he could raise a holler, and Ben's whole plan depended on getting at
> 10 least a two-hour start.
>
> It was a good plan. Ben had figured it all out after he'd got his brains unscrambled back there in Los Angeles County Jail. This had taken time, because when they brought Ben in he was raving. A man could go all to pieces over a woman.
>
> It was a good plan, and yet, as he hurried down the street towards Doctor Ridgeway's
> 15 house, Ben couldn't help thinking about all the things that could go wrong. The guy whose clothes he had taken might wake up and raise the alarm. The doctor might have changed his schedule. This would be fatal. It would leave Ben away out on the end of a limb, ruining his revenge and leaving him only the slim hope of hiding out somewhere in the city.
>
> But luck was with him. The doctor's big black sedan was parked out in front of the house,
> 20 and it was still only twenty minutes past nine. Ben made sure he was unobserved, and then he opened the back door of the car and squeezed in, doubling up his big body so that he was out of sight on the floor. It was cramped in there, the floor of the car was gritty against his hands and his cheek, but now that Ben was so close to success, minor discomforts didn't really bother him.
> 25 After five minutes of this his back and shoulder ached like fury. He thought about Doctor Ridgeway, to get his mind off it. He wondered if the wound had left a scar on Doctor Ridgeway's face. The thought that he might have marred that handsome face permanently was pleasing to Ben. It was the next best thing to putting a bullet clean through his head, which Ben would have done if he hadn't had too many drinks in him at the time.
> 30 A door slammed up at the house. Ben froze. Hurrying footsteps approached the car. In spite of the tightness in his throat, Ben had a momentary feeling of satisfaction. Everything was working according to plan. The doctor was supposed to be at the hospital by ten o'clock, and he was right on schedule. […]
>
> From: Ray Darby, *According to plan*, 1952

a) *Underline or mark some good examples in the text of tenses that belong to the past tense sequence. Explain in the box below how these tenses are used.* → D

Tense	Examples	Use
simple past		
past progressive		
past perfect simple		
conditional		
conditional with *could/might*		
conditional perfect conditional perfect with *might*		

Talking about the past

b) *Answer the questions, keeping to verbs belonging to the past tense sequence.* → D

1. When Ben Wayne paid the taxi driver, he was "careful to keep his face averted and the hat pulled low over his eyes." Why? _____

2. What had happened at the jail that evening? _____

3. What were Ben's hopes and worries as he made his way to the doctor's house? _____

4. What did he do when he arrived there? _____

5. What thoughts went through his head while he was waiting? _____

6. What do you think had happened some time earlier between Ben and the doctor? What do you think the reason might have been? _____

> **Tip**
> When the time relationship is clear from the context, the **past tense** is often used instead of the (longer) **past perfect** form: *As soon as they **got** to the station, the train arrived.*

c) **Creative writing:** *Continue the story, keeping to the past tense sequence.* → D
Start like this: As soon as the doctor (had) got in and started the car …

13 He would lie there for hours …

Read this extract from The Loop, *a novel about the trouble caused in a small Rocky Mountain ranching town when wolves come down into the valley. Luke, 18, the son of one of the ranchers, loves to watch the family of wolves he discovers by chance up in the hills several months before the trouble starts …*

He would lie there for hours at a time, sometimes seeing none, sometimes all of them. As the meadow filled with flowers, Luke watched the pups chasing bees and butterflies and learning how to hunt mice and it was often so comical he found it hard not to laugh out loud. Sometimes when their mother or their father lay dozing in the sun, the pups would
5 stalk them, creeping on their bellies through the lush, long grass. Luke was sure the parents knew what was going on and were just playing along, pretending to be asleep. When they got real close, the pups would pounce and everything went crazy and the whole pack would go chasing around the meadow, tumbling and nipping each other and the game would go on and on until they all collapsed in one big, exhausted heap of wolf.
10   And witnessing this, Luke would silently say a little prayer, not to God, of whose existence he'd had scant evidence so far, but to whoever or whatever decided these things, pleading that the wolves would be smart enough to stay up there where they were safe and not venture down to the valley.
From: Nicholas Evans, *The Loop*, 1998

2 **pup** a young dog (or wolf)

First mark the examples of habitual activities in the text and find the one example of **would** *as a* conditional *form. Then read the sentences below, deciding which of them contain* **would** *as a* conditional *form (C), and which contain* **would** *to express* habitual activities *in the past (H).* → C

1. Luke hoped that the wolves would not come down into the valley. (____)
2. Nobody would ever know he had seen them. (____)
3. Every spring, when the snow had melted, Luke would ride up into the mountains. (____)
4. He knew that if his father saw any wolves on the ranch he would kill them. (____)
5. Whenever he went up into the hills, he wondered whether he would see the pups. (____)
6. The whole family would often sit together by the fire on winter evenings. (____)
7. Whenever his father talked about wolves, Luke would keep quiet and say nothing. (____)

Talking about the past

14 Error spotting: The race for the South Pole

This text is meant to be written in the past tense sequence. 22 mistakes have been made with the verb forms. Find them, mark them and correct them, in the space provided in the margin. → C, D

By 1900, much of the world had already been explored, but nobody has yet been to the Poles. In 1910, after news was arriving that Robert Peary of the US Navy had already been reaching the North Pole, a British team of explorers, led by Captain Robert Scott, wanted to be the first at the South Pole. Scott and his men set sail in June 1910, but soon after they
5 have left, Scott had received a telegram from Roald Amundsen, a Norwegian explorer who also just headed for the South Pole. He wanted Scott to know that he now had competition.
   Scott's expedition was carefully planned, but the equipment he and his team had decided to use was not suitable for the harsh conditions: he did not realise that their clothes will not protect them adequately from the bitter cold and that the ponies they had brought with
10 them to pull the sledges were too heavy and slow.
   Before setting off through the snow, Scott and his men were spending months at their base camp, where they have been waiting for the long, dark polar winter to end. By January 1912, a small team was ready to begin the last stretch of the journey, but after a while the team's progress was so slow that eventually the ponies have to be shot because they had
15 got stuck in the snow. Now the men were being forced to pull the sledges through the snow themselves. When Scott and his four companions finally have reached the South Pole on 17th January, they were bitterly disappointed: there in the snow, a small Norwegian flag already flew in the wind. In a small tent left there by the Norwegian team, they were finding a note for Scott, saying that Amundsen and his men would have arrived there on 14th
20 December – over a month before them!
   With heavy hearts, Scott and his friends, who until then have always hoped that they were the first at the Pole, began their return journey, badly frostbitten and exhausted. But it ended in tragedy. One of the five men collapsed and died when they still had over 400 miles in front of them. Another, believing that he was slowing the others down because he was so
25 ill, walked out of their tent during a blizzard and has never been seen again. But his heroic suicide was of no use to his friends. The dead bodies of the other three men were being discovered by a search party in November 1912 – only eleven miles short of safety.
   If Scott and his companions would have used husky dogs to pull their sledges, like Amundsen did, they had been able to travel faster, and their chances of returning alive had
30 been very much greater.

1. _____
2. _____
3. _____
4. _____
5. _____
6. _____
7. _____
8. _____
9. _____
10. _____
11. _____
12. _____
13. _____
14. _____
15. _____
16. _____
17. _____
18. _____
19. _____
20. _____
21. _____
22. _____

15 Nelson Mandela: A short biography

Use the short notes below as a basis for a biographical text about Nelson Mandela. Naturally you should use the past tense sequence, integrating subordinate clauses of various kinds where suitable. → C, D

1918:	Born in Qunu, Eastern Cape, South Africa.
1944:	First becomes active for the ANC (African National Congress), a black nationalist movement established in 1914.
1948–90:	Under the apartheid system, the white government in South Africa makes non-whites live in separate areas; non-whites cannot vote, own land, travel or work without permits.
1960:	ANC banned; as its leader, Mandela decides the only way to fight against apartheid is to use violence.
1962:	Mandela arrested.
1963:	Tried in court for plotting to overthrow government.
June 1964:	Together with seven others, sentenced to life imprisonment (Robben Island Prison).
1982:	Transferred to Pollsmoor Prison; during years in prison, Mandela is seen as most significant black leader in South Africa; his courage never fails, and even from his prison cell he manages to befriend and educate his oppressors.
1988:	Spends 70th birthday in prison; anti-apartheid concert held at Wembley Stadium in London.
1990:	Mandela finally released after 27 years of prison; end of apartheid.
1993:	Nobel Peace prize; leads ANC, now reformed, into power in peace and partnership with the former racist parties of South Africa.
May 1994:	Aged 77, Mandela becomes President of South Africa; first black president ever, in first democratic elections.
June 1999:	Steps down, but continues to work for peace and equal rights for all people; one of his goals: to give education to every child in the world.
2008:	Party in Hyde Park, London, to celebrate 90th birthday.

Talking about the future

A Different tenses to express future meaning

In English, you can refer to future actions and events in several different ways.
Which of the different tenses and aspects you choose depends on the point of view you want to express. You can use the following tenses:

Tense	Example
going-to future	Are you **going to play** tennis tomorrow?
will future	We**'ll play** if the weather is nice.
present progressive	We**'re starting** at 3 o'clock.
future progressive	We**'ll** only **be playing** for an hour or so.
future perfect	We**'ll have finished** before five o'clock.
simple present	The concert **starts** at 6, **doesn't** it?

B Basic future tenses

Basic rules

The going-to future

The *going-to* future describes what someone wants to do in the future. It expresses a **plan** or an **intention.**

*Are you **going to do** a gap year after school? No, I**'m going to work** in a holiday camp for a couple of months. Then I**'m going to start** university.*

The *going-to* future can also be used when the speaker is **sure** that something will happen in the future – because there are already **signs** that indicate this (the brighter weather, the traffic jam).

*It's brightening up, look! The sun**'s going to come** out in a moment.
Damn this traffic jam! We**'re going to miss** our flight, I'm afraid.*

The will future

The *will* future describes something that is **certain to happen** in the future. The speaker cannot influence these states or events (like the weather or someone's age).

*Most of the south of England and Wales **will have** another sunny day tomorrow. It **won't be** quite so warm in the north.
I**'ll be** 18 at the end of May..*

The *will* future is used after certain verbs *(to hope, to expect, to be sure etc.)* and with adverbs like *probably, perhaps, possibly* etc. In this case it expresses a **supposition**.

*I'm sure we**'ll enjoy** our day at Wimbledon. Let's hope we**'ll see** some really exciting matches! There**'ll** probably **be** masses of other people there.*

You can also use the *will* future when you make a **spontaneous decision**, or offer to help someone, without having planned to do this beforehand.

*There's an awful mess in here! – I**'ll help** you to clear it up.
I**'ll give** you my phone number. – Wait, I**'ll write** it down.*

In realistic **conditional sentences** the *will* future often appears in the main clause.

*I**'ll tell** her if I see her tonight.*

In the same way the *will* future is used in main clauses after or before adverbial clauses with *when, as soon as* or *until*.

*We**'ll call** you as soon as we get home.*

Tip

Do not use the *will* **future** in if-clauses and in adverbial clauses with *when, as soon as* or *until*.

Talking about the future

Basic rules

The present progressive with future meaning

You use the **present progressive** when you talk about **arrangements** that have been made for the future. It is often used with time adverbials like *tomorrow, this weekend, on Monday, next week* etc. These 'future' adverbials make it clear that the verb form refers to the future and not to the present.

Luke and Rebecca **are having** a big party on Saturday.
They**'re** celebrating their birthdays together.
Are you **going**?

When **is** your sister **getting** married?
– Next month!

The simple present with future meaning

The **simple present** can be used for future events when those **events** have been **officially fixed**. It normally refers to the exact times given in timetables and programmes. Therefore it is sometimes called the *timetable future*. It is often used with the verbs *arrive, begin, leave, start* and *end*.

When **do** the summer holidays **start**?
– On 26th July.

Our flight **leaves** at 11.30. And as far as I remember, we **arrive** in Athens at about three in the afternoon.

1 *Will* future? Present progressive?

Choose the form that is most suitable in these short dialogues. → A, B

1. I wonder what the weather _____ (be) like next weekend. – Why? _____ you _____ (do) something exciting? – In a way, yes! Ann and I _____ (go) sailing on Windermere with her two brothers. – Sounds great! And according to the weather forecast, you _____ (probably – be) lucky. They say it _____ (stay) warm and sunny over the next few days.

2. Hey, it's Bill's party tonight! What _____ you _____ (wear)? – I think perhaps I _____ (put on) the new top I got last week – with black jeans. – Oh, yeah, that _____ (look) good, I'm sure!

3. I want to make a cake this evening, but there's not enough flour. – I _____ (get) some for you, don't worry. I _____ (meet) Jack at the new coffee bar in half an hour, so I _____ (be) near the supermarket anyway. – Thanks! – That's OK, it _____ (not take) me long. I _____ (be) back here by 5.30 at the latest.

4. I'm afraid I _____ (not have) time to come round on Sunday after all. My grandparents _____ (come) here for the day, and we _____ (take) them out. We _____ (have) a big slap-up meal at the Victoria Hotel! – Oh? _____ you _____ (celebrate) something? – Yes, my grandmother's birthday – she _____ (be) 75.

5. Do you think we _____ (see) Josh at the barbecue on Saturday? – I don't suppose so. He _____ (fly) to the States on Sunday, don't forget. His mum _____ (drive) him to the airport in the early morning, as far as I remember. – You're right. So I expect he _____ (be) too busy to come.

Talking about the future

2 Which fits best?

Decide which forms are suitable. Cross out the ones you think are wrong. → A, B

1. What (do you do / are you going to do) when (you'll leave / you leave) school? – Well, after my gap year (I'll probably go / I probably go) to university. But I haven't decided yet what subjects (I'm studying / I'm going to study).

2. Can you help me with this Maths problem? – (I'm trying / I'll try)! Show me how far you've got with it, and (I'm going to see / I'll see) what I can do. If (there's / there'll be) a mistake somewhere, I expect (I find / I'll find) it all right.

3. Hurry up, John, or (we're missing / we'll miss) the beginning of the film. – When (is it starting / does it start)? – 8.15. Come on, (we'll be late / we're late) if we (won't leave / don't leave) now. – OK, (I'll read / I'm reading) the rest of these e-mails later!

4. Look at the snow! (We're having / we're going to have) a white Christmas this year! – Sounds romantic, but if it (is going on / goes on) snowing like this, (there'll be / there's) chaos on the roads on Christmas Eve. And (we go / we're going) up north to stay with my grandparents.

3 What's that in English?

Translate these sentences into English. Be careful with the verb forms. → A, B

1. Helen kommt am Freitag in Stuttgart an. Holst du sie am Flughafen ab? – Ja, natürlich!

2. Die Straßen sind morgen früh ganz sicher glatt. Ich glaube, ich fahre mit dem Zug zur Arbeit.

3. Wenn wir am Wochenende Zeit haben, besuchen wir dich.

4. Wie kommen wir denn heute Abend nach Hause? – Ich rufe meine Eltern an, wenn die Party zu Ende geht.

5. Was machen wir denn mit den Erdbeeren da? – Ich mache ein tolles Dessert: ‚Eton Mess'! Das schmeckt euch bestimmt! Moment mal, ich zeige euch das Rezept.

6. Schau mal die Wolken an! Es fängt gleich an zu regnen. Stellst du dein Fahrrad in die Garage? Sonst wird es nass. – Laut Wetterbericht scheint aber morgen wieder die Sonne. Vielleicht haben wir also doch noch Glück mit unserer Fahrradtour.

Tip

In German you generally use **Präsens** when you talk about future events:
Wir treffen uns am Freitagabend.

In English, however, the **simple present** is very rarely used when talking about the future. Apart from timetable events, you normally use different future forms:

Wir treffen uns am Freitagabend.
→ *We're going to meet on Friday evening. / We're meeting on Friday evening.*

Wir treffen uns am Freitagabend, wenn es dir recht ist.
→ *We'll meet on Friday evening if it suits you OK.*

Talking about the future

4 Two uses of the *going-to* future

Explain the difference in meaning between the uses of the going-to future in the two cartoons. → A, B

"Watch the dog. I'm going to do my can opener impression."

"Hop in – I think we're going to get a push."

impression *hier:* Imitation, Nummer

5 What's going to happen?

Look at each photo carefully. Think about the situation. Then explain what you think the consequences are going to be. Then write a sentence for each picture. → A, B

_____
_____

_____
_____

_____
_____

_____
_____

_____
_____

_____
_____

Talking about the future

C Other future forms

Basic rules

The future progressive

The **future progressive** describes an activity in progress at a certain time in the future (This time next month..., When you are ...).

You can also use the **future progressive** to express what is expected to happen in the future. This is very likely to happen whether it's been planned or not.

When you ask someone about their plans and intentions, the **future progressive** sounds less direct and more tactful than the **going-to future** or the **present progressive**.

This time next month I'll be flying to Australia. When you are on holiday in France, I'll be working for an English company in Melbourne.

I've just had an e-mail from the Wilsons. They'll be coming on Friday. I expect they'll be staying here over the weekend.

Will you be seeing Naomi on Saturday?

The future perfect

The **future perfect** expresses that an activity or an event will be completed by a certain time in the future. This point in time is often indicated by time adverbials (*By the end of July*...) or by an adverbial clause of time (*When we get back*...).

By the end of this year we'll have moved into our new house on Cambridge Avenue. When our cousins from the US come to stay, John will already have gone back to boarding school.

6 World record for teenage sailor?

In June 2008, Zac Sunderland, a 16-year-old boy from Los Angeles, set off on an attempt to become the youngest person ever to sail round the world alone. Before he left, he appeared in an interview on television.

Write the interview, using information from the box. Form questions and appropriate answers, with the help of suitable future forms wherever possible. → A, B, C

> **Tip**
> You can also talk about future plans with verbs like *hope, plan, expect, be (un)likely to, be sure to, look forward to,* etc.

Length of journey at sea?	Probably one year.
Route?	Across dangerous waters (Pacific, Indian and Atlantic Oceans).
Length of periods spent alone at sea?	Between 4 and 6 weeks.
Stops?	Planned at suitable places around the world.
Deadline for return?	By January 2010, to break world record.
Personal expectations?	Amazing adventure, seeing different places, meeting new people, being alone at sea.
School work?	All books needed for 1 school year on board; tests via e-mail to be sent to mother for grading; important to finish high school after one more year.

Talking about the future

7 Error spotting: Talking about holidays

In most of these sentences, unsuitable verb forms have been used. (Only two are correct!) Identify the 'wrong' forms, cross them out and replace them by forms that fit the 'intentions' of the speakers. → A, B, C

1. Do you go away on holiday this summer? – Yes, we go to the Channel Islands.

2. We stay at a little hotel called 'La Tour' on the east coast of Guernsey. By this time next week we've arrived – and, hopefully, I'll lie on the beach!

3. 'La Tour'? Will you be staying at a French-speaking hotel, then? – Oh, no! But maybe we're meeting some French people on the island. I'm telling you all about it when we'll get back.

4. Will you have gone to Jersey, too? – Not this time. But we're going to spend a day on Sark. I'm sure my mother is enjoying that – no cars on the island! So we probably explore the island on foot or hire bikes.

8 Before the river trip

In 'Deliverance', an American novel told from the point of view of Ed, a graphics consultant, four men set out from a small Southern town for a three-day camping and canoe trip. In this extract from the first chapter, they are together in a bar, looking at a map and talking about their plans.

a) *First read the text carefully, marking any passages that refer to **the river**, to **the trip** Lewis is planning for them, to **the feelings** the other three men have about it, and to **the arrangements** they make for the coming weekend.* → A, B

> "When they take another survey and rework this map," Lewis said, "all this in here will be blue. The dam at Aintry has already been started, and when it's finished next spring, the river will back up fast. This whole valley will be under water. But right now it's wild. And I *mean* wild; it looks like something up in Alaska. We really ought to go up there before the
> 5 real estate people get hold of it."
> I leaned forward, trying to visualize the land as Lewis said it was at that moment, unvisited and free. I looked around the bar and then back into the map, picking up the river where we would enter it. A little way to the south-west the paper blanched.

29

Talking about the future

"Does this mean it's higher here?" I asked.

"Yes," Lewis said. "It must run through a gorge or something. But we can get through that in a day, easy. And the water should be good, in that part especially."

I didn't have much idea what good meant in the way of water, but for it to seem good to Lewis it would have to meet some very definite standards.

Bobby Trippe was there, across from me. I knew him least well of the others at the table, but I liked him a good deal, even so. He was pleasantly cynical.

"They tell me that this is the kind of thing that gets hold of middle-class householders every once in a while," Bobby said. "But most of them just lie down till the feeling passes. It's the old idea that you're going to get yourself in shape, one of these days. Just like you were when you were on the B-team in high school. Some few people may jog, once in a while. But who runs sprints? Who goes down rivers?"

"Well, you've got a chance to go down one," Lewis said. "The chance is coming up this weekend, if you can get Friday off. Either Ed and I will go, or we all four can go. But you have to let me know right now, so I can get the other canoe."

I liked Lewis; I could feel myself getting caught up again in his capricious enthusiasms that had already taken me bow-hunting with him. I usually went with him whenever he asked me. I had a bow that he helped me pick out, and it was enjoyable walking in the woods with Lewis, when the weather was good, as it usually is in our part of the South in hunting season. I had a good feeling about this trip. After so much shooting at paper images of deer, it was exciting to think of encountering a real one.

"How, exactly, do we get to the river in the first place?" Drew Ballinger asked.

"There's a little town up here, just past the high ground," Lewis said, "name of Oree. We can put in there and come out in Aintry a couple of days later. If we get on the water late Friday, we can be back here the middle of Sunday afternoon, maybe in time for the last half of the pro game on TV."

"There's one thing that bothers me," Drew said. "We don't really know what we're getting into. There's not one of us knows a damned thing about the woods, or about rivers. I can't even row a boat straight, much less paddle my own or anybody else's canoe. What business have I got up there in those mountains?"

"Listen," Lewis said, "you'll be in more danger on the four-lane going home tonight than you'd ever be on the river. Somebody might jump the divider. Who knows?"

"I mean," Bobby said, "the whole thing does seem kind of crazy."

"All right," Lewis said. "Let me demonstrate. What are you going to be doing this afternoon?"

"Well," Bobby thought for a minute. "Most likely I'll see a couple of new people about funds. I have to draw up some papers and get them notarized."

"How about you, Drew?"

"See some more route salesmen. […]"

"Ed?"

"Oh," I said. "Take some photographs for Kitts Textile Mills."

"Too bad," Lewis said. He had made his point without saying anything about the afternoon. He looked around the bar, waiting for the other two to decide.

"Well, well," he said. "What about it?"

"I'll go," Drew said, "if I can bring a Martin along."

"Sure, bring it," Lewis said. "It would be kind of good to hear, way off up in there."

"OK, fellow primitives," Bobby said. "But I insist on some creature comforts. Namely liquor."

"Bring all you like," Lewis said. "In fact, the sensation of going down white water half-drunk is not to be missed."

"You taking your bow, Lewis?" I asked.

"You know it," he said. "And if one of us stabs a deer we can eat the meat."

It sounded fine to me, though I knew it would be poaching, this early in the fall. But I also knew Lewis would do what he said.

"Can you get your car, Drew?" Lewis asked, as we stood up together.

"Sure," he said.

"Ed and I'll meet you-all early Friday, around six-thirty, where Will's Ferry Road runs into the four-lane, at the big new Will's Plaza Shopping Centre. I'll call Sam Steinhauser this evening and see what shape his canoe's in. Most of the other stuff I've got. Wear tennis shoes. Bring liquor and an open mind."

We went.

From: James Dickey, *Deliverance*, 1970 (abridged)

---

39 **four-lane** [ˈfɔːleɪn] *vierspurige Schnellstraße* • 40 **jump the divider** [dʒʌmp ðə dɪˈvaɪdə] *die Sicherheitsbarriere durchbrechen* • 52 **Martin**: a type of guitar • 59 **poaching** *wildern*

Talking about the future

b) *Now try to imagine a dialogue between Ed, the narrator, and Martha, his wife, later that evening. Fill in Ed's part of the dialogue, using suitable forms of the future where appropriate. (Remember: You can also refer to the future with verbs such as: want to, hope to, expect to, plan to, be worried about, look forward to, etc.)* → A, B

Martha: You say this river is somewhere up in the north-east part of the state? But Ed, why do you have to go now? It's September and there may be fog up there. Can't the trip wait till next spring?

Ed: _____
_____

Martha: OK, I get the picture. But where exactly are you going to get on the river? It sounds so wild up there! And when in heaven's name do you expect to get back?

Ed: _____
_____

Martha: If all goes well, you mean! Ed, frankly, I'm worried. What about that gorge Lewis told you about? Won't the water there be terribly rough? Be honest with me, Ed!

Ed: _____
_____

Martha: Let's hope for the best, then. But what about the other two? How do they feel about this trip? Bobby, for example. He doesn't seem much of an outdoor type to me.

Ed: _____
_____

Martha: And Drew? I can't imagine him in a canoe! And yet he's confident about this trip? Come on, Ed! Are you sure Drew wants to come?

Ed: _____
_____
_____

Martha: Well, surely Lewis must admit there's a risk involved. After all, none of you know what it's going to be like on that river. There's always a danger something may happen.

Ed: _____
_____

Martha: Lewis said that?! Hm. And what kind of stuff are you all taking along?

Ed: _____
_____

Martha: I guess I can't stop you going. But don't blame me if you get caught for poaching! So what are your plans for Friday then? Off at the crack of dawn, I guess?

Ed: _____
_____
_____

c) *Although Ed and his friends don't yet know it, they are heading for a horrifying adventure when they go down the river in their canoes. What do you think will happen to them? Discuss ideas in small groups or with a partner, then write the best ones down on a separate piece of paper.*
   – Perhaps they'll … – I think they're going to … → A, B

| rocks? | weather? | wild animals? | snakes? |

| strange people? | accident? |

Tip

'Deliverance', which was on the US bestseller lists for six months, was later made into a film. Watch it if you can get it on DVD, and find out what really happened. The German title is 'Flussfahrt' or 'Beim Sterben ist jeder der Erste'.

Talking about the future

9 Climate change: What will happen?

James Lovelock, a famous British scientist, has been described as 'one of the great thinkers of our time' *(New Scientist)*.
First read the texts below, all extracts from the first chapter of his highly praised book, 'The Revenge of Gaia' (2006), about the possible consequences of global warming.

1.
Science tries to be global and more than a loose collection of separated disciplines, but even those who take a systems-science approach would be the first to admit that our understanding of the Earth system is not much better than a nineteenth century physician's understanding of a patient. But we are sufficiently aware of the physiology of the Earth
5 to realize the severity of its illness. We suspect the existence of a threshold, set by the temperature or the level of carbon dioxide in the air; once this is passed, nothing the nations of the world do will alter the outcome and the Earth will move irreversibly to a new hot state. We are now approaching one of these tipping points, and our future is like that of the passengers on a small pleasure boat sailing quietly above the Niagara Falls, not knowing that
10 the engines are about to fail.

2.
The few things we do know about the response of the Earth to our presence are deeply disturbing. Even if we stopped immediately all further seizing of Gaia's land and water for food and fuel production and stopped poisoning the air, it would take the Earth more than a thousand years to recover from the damage we have already done, and it may be too late
15 even for this drastic step to save us. To recover, even to lessen the consequences of our past errors, will take an extraordinary degree of international effort and a carefully planned sequence for replacing fossil carbon with safer energy sources.

3.
Now that we are over six billion hungry and greedy individuals, all aspiring to a first-world lifestyle, our urban way of life encroaches upon the domain of the living Earth. We are taking
20 so much that it is no longer able to sustain the familiar and comfortable world we have taken for granted. Now it is changing, according to its own internal rules, to a state where we are no longer welcome […] The acceleration of the climate change now under way will sweep away the comfortable environment to which we are adapted.

4.
The time of irreversible adverse change may be so close that it would be unwise to rely
25 on international agreement to save civilization from the consequences of global heating. We have to make decisions based on our national interest. This is neither chauvinist nor selfish: it could be the fastest way to ensure that more and more nations, driven by their own self-interest, act locally over global change. The large emergent nations, India and China, will find it difficult to rein in their use of fossil fuel, as will the USA. We should not wait for
30 international agreement or instruction.

5.
In our small country we have to act now as if we were about to be attacked by a powerful enemy. We have first to make sure our defences against climate change are in place before the attack begins. The most vulnerable places are the cities close to sea level now, and among them are London and Liverpool. First we need to ensure that they are adequately
35 defended for the early stages of the climate war and then be prepared to retreat from them in an orderly way as the floods advance […] We need, most of all, that change of heart and mind that comes to tribal nations when they sense real danger. Only then will we accept the hardships of fuel rationing and firm constraints that an effective defence demands. Our cause will be the defence of our civilization to ward off the chaos that might otherwise
40 overtake us.

---

3 **physician** doctor • 5 **threshold** *Schwelle* • 8 **tipping point** *Umschlagspunkt* • 12 **to seize** to take • 19 **to encroach on** *eingreifen, verletzen* • 20 **to sustain** *erhalten* • 21 **to take for granted** *als selbstverständlich voraussetzen* • 22 **acceleration** *Beschleunigung* • 28 **emergent** *aufstrebend* • 35 **to retreat** to move back or away (from an enemy) • 39 **cause** *Sache, für die man kämpft*

Talking about the future

a) *The problem – as James Lovelock sees it – and how to face it. True or false? Decide which of the following statements coincide with James Lovelock's view. Rewrite those that are 'false', according to what you read in the texts. Otherwise tick the statement (✓).* → A, B, C

1. Although we do not really know much about the way the 'Earth system' works, we suppose we have already passed the 'tipping point' beyond which global warming will be completely out of control. *(text 1)*

2. It is going to be extremely difficult for us to recover from the damage that has already been done. *(text 2)*

3. Fossil carbon will have to be replaced immediately by safer energy sources. *(text 2)*

4. It will not be possible for everybody in the world to enjoy the kind of lifestyle we have become used to in the richer countries, because the Earth will simply not be able to sustain it. *(text 3)*

5. If we want to fight global warming (heating) successfully, we will first have to come to international agreements and keep to them. *(text 4)*

6. One of the first effects of climate change will be that low-lying cities like London and Liverpool will be threatened by flooding. *(text 5)*

7. If we change our attitudes and act in time, it will probably still be possible to avoid hardships such as fuel rationing. *(text 5)*

b) **Your opinion:**
What do you think our world will be like by the middle of the 21st century? What will be happening? What will have changed? First discuss ideas (in groups or with a partner), then write a short paragraph, giving your own predictions. (You can be optimistic ☺ or pessimistic ☹!) Aspects you might consider: lifestyle, e.g. in 'first world countries' (energy, free time, food, health care, education...); life in countries now belonging to the 'third world'; climate change; international relations ... → A, B, C

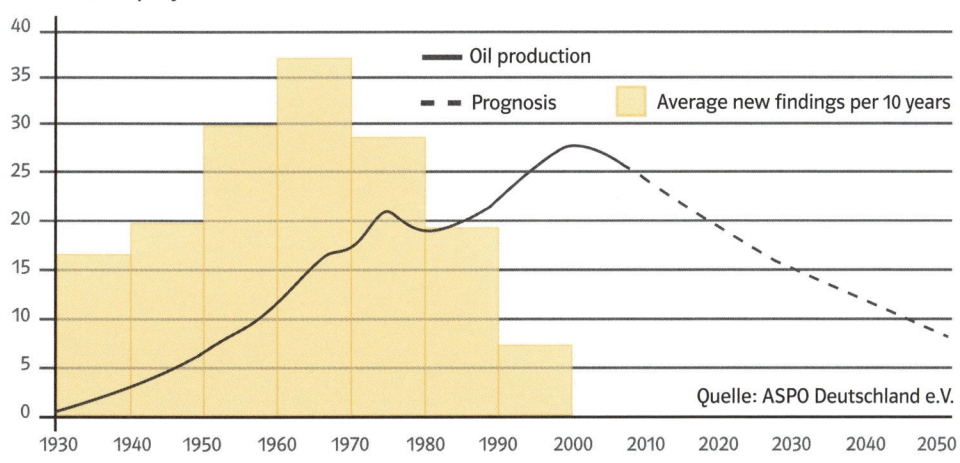

Quelle: ASPO Deutschland e.V.

4 Using modal auxiliaries

A Modal auxiliaries and their meanings

Modal auxiliaries are useful in expressing speech intentions of many different kinds.

Basic rules

Ability (*can, can't, could, couldn't*)

Can (*cannot/can't*) and *could* (*couldn't*) express that someone (or something) is able or unable to do something.
The substitute form is *be able to*.

My parents **can** speak French and a little German. But they **can't** speak Spanish. When they went to Spain on holiday last year, they **couldn't** understand much. Luckily the menus were in Spanish and English, so they **were able to** order meals in restaurants.
Next year they want to go to Scotland. Let's hope they**'ll be able to** understand the Scots OK!

Obligation (*must, needn't, be to, be supposed to, ought to, should*)

Must expresses that something is necessary or should be done. *Needn't* expresses that something is not necessary.
The usual substitute form is *have to*, but *be forced to* and *be required to* are also sometimes used.

I really **must** go now.
I **have to** be home before midnight.
But you **needn't** give me a lift. I can easily walk.
I'**ll have to** do a lot of work tomorrow.

Be supposed to and *be to* refer to what someone else has ordered or instructed.

Are we **supposed to** hand in our essays by the end of this week?
Ms Soames says we'**re not to** copy things word for word from the net.

Should and *ought to* express criticism or moral obligation.

We really **should** get to work on the essays today.
I **ought to** have started mine much earlier.

Possibility (*can, can't, may, might, must, will*)

Can, *could*, *may* and *might* express that something is possible or seems to be possible.

Must and *will* express that the speaker expects something to be certain or very probable.

Excuse me, **can** you tell me the time?
10.15? It **can't** be that late, **can** it?
Must be! Well, it **may** be a bit earlier. My watch **might** be wrong. But it'**ll** be after ten, definitely.

Permission (*may, may not, can, can't, mustn't, be permitted to*)

You use *may* to ask politely for permission.

Mustn't, *can't* and *may not* (more formal) are used to refuse permission. Apart from the substitute form *be allowed to*, you can also use *be permitted to*.

May we look round the cathedral? – No, I'm afraid you **can't** just now, there's a service just starting. You'**ll be allowed to** go in as soon as it's over, of course.
You **mustn't** take photos in here, Judy!
Excuse me, madam, but visitors **are** not **permitted to** smoke in this building.

Willingness

You can use *will* in questions and question tags to ask if someone is willing to do something.
Won't and *wouldn't* express refusal.

Will you come here a moment, please? Help me with the washing machine, **will** you?
It **won't** work. Have I done something wrong?
Mum wanted Jim to do the washing up last night, but he **wouldn't**.

Tip

In spoken English people often use *have got to* instead of *must* or *have to*: *I've got to go now.*

Tip

Be careful with *must*, *mustn't* and *needn't*.

Du musst das tun.
→ *You must do that.*

Du darfst das nicht tun.
→ *You mustn't do that.*

Du brauchst das nicht zu tun.
→ *You needn't do that.*

Tip

Modals are also often used with **perfect forms**:
You should have written. She might have known. We could have done the job.

Tip

The English equivalent of German *Es ist nicht erlaubt, das zu tun*, or *Es ist verboten, das zu tun*, is *You are not allowed to do that.*

Using modal auxiliaries

B Modal auxiliaries and their substitutes

Can, may, must, and *needn't* are the most common *modal auxiliaries.*
May, must and *needn't* can only be used in the *present tense; can* has the *past tense* form *could.*

For all the other tenses you have to use substitutes:

Modal auxiliaries		Substitutes	past	future
can, could	↔	cannot/can't, could not/couldn't	be able to	was/were able to	will be able to
may, can	↔	may not/mustn't, cannot/can't	be allowed to	was/were allowed to	will be allowed to
must	↔	needn't	have to	had to	will have to
needn't			not have to	didn't have to	won't have to

> **Tip**
> The **substitute forms** (especially *be allowed to* and *have to*) are also very often used in the present tense:
> *You're not allowed to smoke in here.*

1 Different situations – different modals

Fill in the different modal auxiliaries. You will sometimes need to use negative forms.
If you think there is more than one possible answer, write the alternative(s) in brackets ( ). → A

1. I _____ read that sign over there. What does it say? – You really
   _____ have your eyes tested! It says "No Smoking".
2. I wonder what we _____ do about the dogs this time when we go away.
   We _____ forget to make arrangements for them in time. – Perhaps we
   _____ ask Mrs Turner to look after them for us. – No, we _____
   do that, she's far too old! She _____ be almost ninety by now.
3. _____ you help me with the cooking today, Jim? – _____ I?
   I'm so busy, Mum! _____ you ask Sue?
4. Do you want me to collect you after the party, Rosie? – It's OK, Dad, you _____
   this time. I _____ easily get the last bus home.
5. There _____ be something wrong with the dishwasher. I've switched it on, but
   it _____ start. – It _____ be a power failure, you never know. I'll
   try switching the lights on … Yes, as I thought! The lights _____ work either.
6. Stop! You _____ throw that magazine away, Tom. – Why not? – There's
   an article in it about mountaineering that Dad _____ want to read. He
   _____ even want to cut it out.
7. I'm so tired! – You _____ go to bed earlier, then.
   Why _____ you always stay up so late? You simply don't get enough sleep, Ben.
   – I know, Dad, you _____ tell me.
8. I'm afraid I _____ pick you up this evening after all, Sam. I wanted to take
   Mum's car, but she _____ let me have it this time. – You _____
   worry, Daniel, we _____ just as easily go by bus.

Using modal auxiliaries

2 At boarding school in the 1960s

*Emma goes to the same boarding school as her grandmother went to in the 1960s. But a lot has changed since those days. This is what Emma's grandmother tells her. Complete the text with suitable forms of **be able to, be allowed to** and **have to**. (In two cases you will need a gerund form.)* → B

"The school rules were very strict in those days, Emma. Upstairs in the dormitories we _____ keep to a 'silence rule'. That meant we _____ talk to each other at all when we went up at bed time. Terrible! But I suppose it was partly so that the younger girls _____ get to sleep without being disturbed. We _____ get up (again without _____ talk to anyone!) at 7.15 in the mornings. OK, we _____ stay in bed an hour longer on Sundays – though we all _____ go to church.

"Like you, we _____ wear uniform, but we _____ wear it in the evenings. We _____ change into our 'home clothes' at teatime every day, which was great! Not surprisingly, though, we _____ wear make-up at all, not even mascara. If anyone came back to school after the holidays with lipstick or nail varnish on, they _____ go and take it off immediately!

"Most people's parents lived quite a distance away, so we _____ see them very often. Even on the weekends when we _____ go out with our parents, we _____ be back by six thirty in the evening for supper.

"But all in all it wasn't so bad. Even then, the school had sixteen tennis courts, so I loved _____ play tennis in the summer term. The food was good, too, and we _____ eat anything we didn't like. The teaching was excellent, of course, and most of us in the Sixth Form did well enough in our A levels to _____ go to university – just like you will, Emma."

dormitory ['dɔːmɪtrɪ] *Schlafsaal* • **Sixth Form** *die oberen zwei Klassen*

3 Natural ways of reacting

Imagine these situations. How would you react? Use auxiliaries to express yourself. → A, B
Example: Your friend can't go to the cinema with you because he's catching up on a whole week's homework. (Express a criticism.)
"You ought to plan things better." / "You mustn't always leave things till the last minute."

1. Your train has arrived and you have to get off – but with a lot of heavy luggage. (*Ask someone help.*) _____

2. A boy at your party wants to drive three girls home, although he's been drinking. (*Mention the risks and the law.*) _____

3. Your friend has found someone's purse on the bus. (*Give advice.*) _____

4. Two girls come onto the beach with their dog, although there's a sign: 'Dog-free zone'. (*Point out the rule.*) _____

5. Your grandparents are always complaining about their big garden. (*Make a suggestion.*) _____

6. A friend is having some trouble with their schoolwork. (*Encourage, and offer your help.*) _____

Using modal auxiliaries

4 When children are left alone at home

a) *First read the text, marking the modal auxiliaries you find as you go along.* → A, B

When is it all right for children to be left on their own? This is a question that causes a lot of uncertainty among parents in Britain, because the law does not state the age at
5 which leaving children alone becomes acceptable. So how are parents supposed to know whether they might get into trouble for leaving their children unsupervised? The fact is that, according to a law made
10 in 1933 called the Children and Young Persons Act, parents can be prosecuted for leaving children alone, especially if the child has suffered as a result. In severe cases of neglect, parents could be given a prison
15 sentence of up to ten years.
Parents are advised that it is best for them to be especially careful about leaving kids alone at home during the school holidays. According to a police spokesman, a child's 20 age cannot always be linked to how responsibly they behave. A child of nine or ten, for example, may be more mature than a fourteen or fifteen-year-old. This means that each child has to be considered 25 individually.
And what about leaving babies and young children in the care of an older brother or sister? In this case it is advisable for parents not to be more than fifteen minutes away. 30 The older child left in charge should know how to contact them and what to do if there is an emergency.

12 **prosecuted** [ˈprɒsɪkjuːtɪd] *strafrechtlich verfolgt*

b) *Use auxiliaries to answer these questions, but don't quote word for word from the text.* → A, B

1. What are the possible consequences for parents who leave their children alone without supervision? _____
   _____

2. Why doesn't the law make it clear when exactly children are responsible enough to be left on their own? _____
   _____

3. What is the best policy when leaving an older child in charge? _____
   _____
   _____

c) *Replace the marked phrases from the text using auxiliaries. The meaning should remain the same.* → A, B

1. the age at which **leaving children alone becomes acceptable**: _____
   _____

2. **it is best for them to** be especially careful: _____

3. know … **what to do** if there is an emergency: _____

d) *Your opinion: Use these sentence parts to help put together eight statements that express your own opinion.* → A, B

Example: In my opinion, very young children should never be left on their own, even for a few minutes.

Generally, parents …	might …
During the holidays, older children …	could …
Children under eight …	should …
If left on their own, young children …	should never .
Teenagers left alone over night …	should have to …
Parents that neglect their children …	should(n't) be allowed to …
Generally, teenagers …	ought to be able to …
Very young children …	…

Using modal auxiliaries

5 What went wrong?

How could you comment on these people's problems? Use perfect forms of auxiliaries (as many different ones as you can). → A

should(n't) have • may (not) have • must have • might have • ought (not) to have • can't have • could have • needn't have

Example: I'm afraid that plant you gave me for my birthday has died!
– Well, maybe you ought to have watered it more often.

1. I sent a Christmas card to an old friend in Bristol, but it was returned with an official label saying 'Not known at this address'.

2. Andy agreed to come round at 7.30, but it's after eight and he's still not here!

3. I wanted to do roast chicken for lunch today, but the bird's still frozen hard!

4. Oh, sorry I didn't come to your party last night. I had too many other things to do.

5. My grandmother always sends me something for my birthday, but there's nothing in the post from her today. Do you think she's forgotten?

6. I can't find my sunglasses, and I've looked everywhere. Where on earth can they be?

7. I'm afraid I couldn't get tickets for us for The Woman in Black after all – they were sold out!

8. Julie and I went for a long walk through the snow yesterday, which was great! But I'm afraid my cold is worse than ever today – I just can't seem to get rid of it.

9. I left the car in a 'no parking' area, I admit. But it was only for ten minutes. And now some stupid traffic warden has given me a ticket!

10. Don't say you've thrown Saturday's paper away?! There was an article in it that I wanted to cut out!

11. I was so afraid I'd fail my driving test, I was shaking all over when I got into the car. But imagine it, I've passed after all!

12. I can't get hold of the Smiths. I've tried to ring them countless times, but nobody goes to the phone.

ticket *Strafzettel*

Using modal auxiliaries

C Equivalents of German 'sollen' (*shall, ought to/should, be to, be supposed to, be said to*)

Basic rules

You can use **Shall** I …? **Shall** we …? when you make a suggestion or when you ask what someone else would like you to do.
Shall is also used in question tags after suggestions with **Let's** …

Should and **ought to** can be used to give advice or to express criticism (see **A: Obligation**)

Be to and **be supposed to** express that something has been decided (by someone else) (see **A: Obligation**).

Be supposed to and **be said to** can be used to express what is assumed as true.

Shall we eat out this evening?
OK, where **shall** we go?
Shall I collect you at 7?

Let's go to Gino's, **shall** we?

We **should** call them and tell them we'll be late.
We **ought to** have left earlier.

Are we **supposed to** read the whole novel?
Students **are not to** remove magazines from the library.

Garlic **is supposed to** be very good for you.
Yes, sure. And **it's said to** protect you from vampires.

> **Tip**
> The English equivalent for *'sollte lieber/besser …'* is *'had better'*.
> Du solltest jetzt besser gehen. → *You'd better go now.*

6 Calvin's Saturday morning

Using modal auxiliaries

a) *Look at what happens to Calvin one Saturday morning. Find sentences that contain examples of modal auxiliaries, and translate them into German. (Mark them first if you wish.)* → C

_____
_____
_____

b) *Complete the sentences with English equivalents of German* sollen. *There is often more than one way of doing this. (Sometimes negative forms are needed.)* → C

| be supposed to | shall | be said to | ought to | should |

1. Calvin's father thinks Calvin _____ spend the whole day watching TV.

2. "What's Calvin doing?" his mother asks his father. "Where is he?" – "In the sitting-room, I guess, dear. _____ I go and have a look?"

3. Calvin gets angry when his father switches the TV off, but his parents have very strict rules and Calvin knows quite well he _____ go out and play when the weather is good. And even on wet weekends he _____ watch TV all day.

4. "Dad _____ have been so strict with us just now! It's so boring out here!" says Calvin to his tiger when they get outside. "What _____ we do, Hobbes?" – "No idea," says Hobbes. "Hey, wait a minute, though. _____ we go over to Susie's place?"

5. "Great idea!" says Calvin. "We _____ have thought of that right away! C'mon, Hobbes!"

6. Soon they're watching TV with Susie. "This is great!" says Calvin. "After all, your childhood days _____ be the happiest days of your life – which they certainly are if you can at least spend your weekends in front of the TV!"

7 Mediation: Brand im Hotel: Was ist zu tun?

Explain these tips for hotel guests in simple English. → A, B, C

These expressions will be useful:

| fire extinguisher | to block | to draw attention to oneself |

Was müssen Gäste beachten, um sich zu schützen?

- Nach dem Einchecken sollte man sich vorsichtshalber darüber informieren, wo die Treppenhäuser, die Fluchtwege und die Feuerlöscher sind. Im Brandfall kann der Rauch die Sicht stark einschränken.
- Die Aufzüge sollten auf keinen Fall benutzt werden. Bei der Flucht muss die Zimmertür sehr vorsichtig geöffnet werden, denn sie könnte sehr heiß sein.
- Wenn Feuer und Rauch ein Entkommen unmöglich machen, ist der Gast gezwungen, im Zimmer zu bleiben. Erst sollte man versuchen, die Türspalten mit feuchten Handtüchern zu verstopfen, damit der Rauch nicht so schnell eindringen kann. Dann sollte man sich am Fenster bemerkbar machen.

Using modal auxiliaries

8 Not as expected

a) *Look at the cartoon and explain the situation.* → A, B, C

b) *Think of other situations in which one person doesn't fulfil another's expectations. Choose one of the situations and write a dialogue between the two people in it.* → A, B, C

9 An exchange student is surprised

Underline the correct forms. → A, B, C

When I was in the US, I was amazed how different some of the laws are from what I'd expected. I'd known that young people (are supposed to/can/should) get their driver's license early, but hadn't realised that some states actually (force/allow/require) kids to drive with a learner's permit at the age of 14 or 15! On the other hand, young Americans (needn't/won't/are
5 not permitted to) buy alcohol or drink in public until they are 21. This rule applies nationwide. It (became illegal/became law/was allowed) in 1984 after a campaign by 'Mothers Against Drunk Driving'.

In Virginia, the state I stayed in, adults (aren't allowed to/should/may) let any guests under 21 drink alcohol in their home. This meant that when Rick celebrated his 18th birthday, we
10 (ought to/weren't required to/had to) keep to soft drinks only. Not even beer (was required/ was permitted/was forbidden)! I knew his parents had some in the house, but they (won't/ shouldn't/wouldn't) let me touch it. They said if the police found out, they (might have to/ would have had to/had been forced to) go to jail! And I had thought America (should/was to/ was supposed to) be the "land of the free"!
15 But if only the US gun laws were stricter! In my opinion, they (are supposed to/ought to/are required to) be!

10 Say it in English

Find the best way to express these ideas in English. → A, B, C

1. Du musst nicht mit uns mitkommen. _____
2. Soll das ein Witz sein? _____
3. Das darf man nicht zu ernst nehmen. _____
4. Was soll das bedeuten? _____
5. Du brauchst dich nicht zu entschuldigen. _____
6. Wir sollten die Polizei rufen. _____
7. Das hätten Sie nicht tun sollen! _____
8. Sollen wir morgen schwimmen gehen? _____
9. Du solltest jetzt besser aufhören! _____
10. Sie müssen das doch gewusst haben! _____

5 Using the passive

A Active and passive voice

There is a difference in viewpoint between *active* sentences and *passive* sentences: *Active* sentences stress who or what does something. In *passive* sentences the activity itself is in the foreground. The emphasis is on what is done, while the 'doer' is either obvious, unimportant or unknown.
The *passive* is often used in factual and historical texts, in newspaper articles and reports.

Active	Passive
Thousands of workers **built** the Empire State Building in record time.	The Empire State Building **was built** between 1930 and 1931 – in just over a year

B Forms of the passive

The same rules apply to the use of the passive tenses as to the active tenses. In the **simple** form, all the tenses of the active voice can also be formed in the passive. But there are only two tenses that can be used in the **progressive** form: **present progressive** and **past progressive.**

Basic rules

The **simple present** is used when something is often, regularly or never done. It is also used to state facts.	Millions of tons of oil **are burnt** every day.
You use the **present progressive** to describe what is happening at the moment and is still going on.	Large underwater oilfields **are being explored**.
The **present perfect** is used to stress the effect of a past action on the present. It can also express that a state began in the past and still continues.	A few new methods of conserving energy **have been discovered**. Nuclear energy **has been used** since the 1950s.
The **simple past** is used to stress that an event came to an end in the past.	During the Industrial Revolution a lot of coal **was mined** in Britain.
The **past progressive** describes what was in progress at a certain time in the past.	Luckily the weather stayed calm while the gigantic new oilrig **was being towed** out to sea.
The **past perfec**t expresses that something happened before another activity or event in the past.	Before the steam engine was invented, only wind, water and muscle power **had been used**.
The **will future** is used to predict events in the future.	More and more energy **will be needed** in the future.
The **infinitive** is used after modal auxiliaries and in all other cases where an infinitive is needed.	Alternative technologies **must be developed**. In Britain, sunlight is too unreliable **to be considered** as an efficient source of energy.

Tip

In English, verbs and prepositions are closely linked. They also stay together in passive sentences:
You *haven't paid for* those books. ➡ Those books *haven't been paid for*.
We'*ll deal with* the problem. ➡ The problem *will be dealt with*.

Tip

In spoken English you often come across the passive with *get*. This form indicates that an event is unexpected or unintended:
The cyclist got badly hurt in the accident.
Don't forget to lock your bike. It might get stolen.

Other passive forms are:

conditional	The bridge **would be built** now if the town had enough money.
future perfect	In ten years the bridge **will have been** built.
conditional perfect	The bridge **would have been built** ages ago if the town council hadn't been against it.
perfect infinitive	The bridge should **have been built** while there was still enough money.

Using the passive

1 New ideas for the Interstate highway system

Put these sentences together with the correct passive verb forms. → B

1. The US Interstate highway system ___ in the 1950s.
2. Since then more than 47,000 miles of multilane roadways ___ all over the country.
3. Now every major American city ___ in this way.
4. Thus a car culture relying heavily on fossil fuel ___ .
5. Now new ideas for revolutionising these big roads ___ .
6. Popular Light-Rail systems alongside the highways ___ already in some areas.
7. In addition, a new electrical power grid ___ alongside these roads.
8. This way, energy for battery-powered vehicles ___ available.
9. Imagine a system in which electric cars ___ for the day at a Light-Rail station.
10. People will then ride to work while their cars ___ .
11. And, of course, all roadside lights ___ with energy from solar panels.

A	can be left
B	could be constructed
C	will be powered
D	have been built
E	was begun
F	are being recharged
G	is connected
H	has been created
I	would be made
J	are being used
K	are being considered

C The use of the *by-agent* in passive sentences

Basic rules

Very often the person or thing that causes an action to happen is not mentioned in passive sentences – because the event itself is in the foreground and the 'doer' is obvious, unimportant or unknown. But when it is important to mention the person or thing that causes the action, a **by-agent** is used.
The **object** of the active sentence corresponds to the **subject** of the passive sentence.
The **by-agent** corresponds to the **subject** of the active sentence.

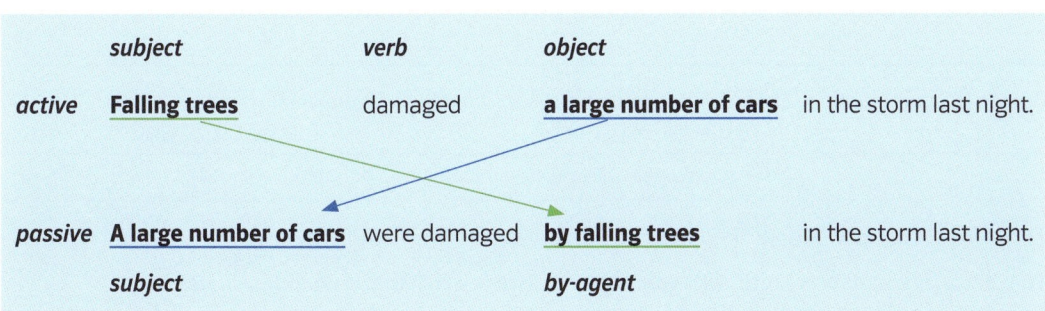

2 Who did it?

Read the passive sentences below and decide: → A, C

Is the 'doer':
- obvious? (If so, add a full stop and mark: A.)
- unimportant? (If so, add a full stop and mark: B.)
- unknown? (If so, add a full stop and mark: C.)
- important? (If so, add a suitable by-agent.)

1. Last night our house was broken into _____
2. The main part in the new film will be played _____
3. A number of trees were blown down in the storm _____
4. Our new school hall was opened in 2007 _____
5. When I was in hospital, I was visited _____
6. My bike has been stolen _____
7. The man that took the money has now been arrested _____
8. The corner shop at the end of our road is owned _____

Using the passive

3 Football stars join the fight against knife crime

Put the active structures (marked in the text in italics) into the passive. Use a by-agent only when it seems necessary. → B, C

Knife crime, especially in big cities, is a serious problem in Britain. Sadly, *it often involves young people.* _____

_____

But in August 2008 *three England football stars joined the British Government and police*

_____

_____

_____

in the fight against knife crime. *The three celebrities, Rio Ferdinand, David James and David Beckham, launched a completely new anti-knife campaign.*

_____

_____

_____

They called the campaign 'It Doesn't Have to Happen'. _____

_____

"A lot of young people simply don't listen to us," said a police spokesman, *"so they aren't registering our message about knives.* _____

_____

But we think it's likely that *children and teenagers will listen to popular sports stars."*

_____

_____

The Home Secretary added: "People who think that carrying a knife makes them safer are wrong. The fact is, if you have a knife with you, there is always a risk that *someone will use it; they may even use it against you."* _____

_____

During the two months before the launch of the new campaign, *police had stopped and searched over 50,000 people* _____

_____

in ten 'problem areas'. *They had seized 1,600 knives and made more than 2,500 arrests.*

_____

_____

In future, according to newspaper reports, it seemed likely that *the Government would use metal detectors* _____

in Britain's toughest schools.

Using the passive

4 Our disappearing forests

Fill in the verbs in the passive, using the correct form. → B

1. Before the impact of humans, over 80 % of the world's land _____ (cover) by forests.
2. Since those days, this area _____ (reduce) from 80 % to less than 30 %.
3. In the temperate zones of the 'Developed World', this is less of a problem, because new trees _____ (plant) all the time.
4. But in tropical regions, about 1 % of the forests _____ (lose) each year. (This is an area about the same size as the whole of Britain!)
5. If this trend _____ (not stop), tropical forests will have disappeared altogether by the end of this century.
6. If we allowed this to happen, the amazing diversity of natural life they contain _____ (lose) for ever.
7. Most of the cleared forest area in these tropical regions _____ (use) for agriculture to supply cattle food – not only for meat-loving countries in the West.
8. In fact, in those Latin American countries where most trees _____ (already – cut down), the demand for meat products is now even higher than in North America.
9. Another reason for clearing forests is that more and more space _____ (require) for towns, cities and roads.
10. And, to make things worse, the population in tropical regions _____ (expect) to continue growing …

D Verbs with two objects in passive sentences

Verbs like **give, offer, promise, send, show** etc. can have two objects:
They've offered him a job.
In this sentence *him* is the **indirect object** and *a job* is the **direct object**.
Passive sentences with these verbs can be formed in two different ways:

Basic rules

Passive 1 (personal passive)	Passive 2
Viola **was given** *the part* of a fairy in 'A Midsummer Night's Dream'.	No, *the part* **wasn't offered** to Trish. It **was** definitely **given** to Viola. *The role of Bottom* **was given** to the funniest student in the drama group.
The students **were shown** *two film versions* of the play before the rehearsals started.	*Two film versions of the play* **were shown** to the students that wanted to take part in the rehearsals.
In most cases a person *(Viola, the students)* is used as the **subject** of the passive sentence. That is why this type is called the **personal passive**. (When translating into German it is often best to use sentences with '*man*' or '*jemand*'.)	If a thing *(the part, two film versions)* becomes the subject of the passive sentence, the **person (the indirect object)** is put at the end of the sentence with the preposition **to**. This is normally only the case if the indirect object is stressed – or if it is particularly long.

45

Using the passive

5 Before you buy a new puppy

What is puppy trafficking?

We might like to think that if we buy a puppy, it would have been brought up by its mother in a warm loving atmosphere with its brothers and sisters, before we bring it home to live with us. However, this is often not the case.

The RSPCA recently warned that many puppies are actually bred on large 'farms', where there could be hundreds of puppies and mothers in bare, miserable cages. The puppies are then driven, maybe hundreds of miles, to the place where they are going to be sold. This is what the charity calls 'Puppy Trafficking'.

Puppies treated in this way are in danger of becoming ill, as often they are not given the medical treatment that all puppies need to protect them against illnesses.

Where are these puppies sold?

They could be sold anywhere! If you are looking for a puppy, you might look in a newspaper, or on the internet, or go to a pet shop. And it is possible that a puppy found through any of these places has been 'trafficked'.

"Lots of people selling puppies look after them very well," said Justine Pannett, campaigner for the RSPCA. "But people who are buying puppies should know exactly where their new pet has come from and how it has been treated, and that's not always easy."

Undercover investigations

To try and discover how bad the problem is, the RSPCA sent undercover inspectors to buy puppies from six pet shops. Out of the six, two of the dogs were found to have life-threatening illnesses.

The other four dogs were all healthy, although two of them had problems with their behaviour – another symptom of puppies that have been trafficked.

"It is very important for puppies to be socialized – which means shown the world around them, and meeting other dogs and people. If this doesn't happen – which is usually the case with 'trafficked' puppies – then this could lead to problems later on, such as being scared of everything, or even fighting."

From: *First News*, August 22, 2008

Hector was bought from a pet shop in London as part of our undercover operation. A Yorkshire Terrier who cost £475, Hector was found to be possessive about food – a behavioural difficulty which could be a result of being trafficked. This is being dealt with though, and he has been successfully rehomed.

> **Tip**
> *Puppies treated in this way* is an example of a **past participle** used to shorten a relative clause with a passive verb form: *Puppies which have been treated in this way*.
> You'll find more about the use of **participles** in Chapters 7 and 9.

> **Tip**
> *… being trafficked* is a passive form of the **gerund**. You'll find more about **gerunds** in Chapters 7 and 9.

puppy ['pʌpi]: a young dog • 7 **RSPCA**: Royal Society for the Prevention of Cruelty to Animals

a) *Read the text, marking the passive forms you find as you go along, including the two personal passive forms. Then answer these questions, using passive forms wherever suitable.* → B, C, D

1. If you buy a puppy that has been 'trafficked', what does this mean? What has probably happened to it? _____

2. Why are 'trafficked' puppies likely to become ill? _____

3. What other problems may they have? Why? _____

b) *There is only one example of a by-agent in the text. Find it, and explain why it is important.*
_____

Using the passive

c) *Rephrase **without** using the passive. (Think about a possible subject for the active sentences, e. g. 'an RSPCA worker'.)*

1. Hector was found to be possessive about food. _____
   _____

2. This is being dealt with. _____

3. He has been successfully rehomed. _____
   _____

d) *Complete what some people said when they heard about the problem. Choose from these verbs:*

| take advantage of | pay for | look after | hear of | deal with |

1. "It's so important for animals to _____ properly, especially in the first few weeks."
2. "Puppy trafficking sounds like a fairly recent problem. As far as I know, it _____ certainly never _____ a few years ago."
3. "It seems to me that puppy trafficking should _____ more strictly."
4. "If a puppy becomes ill because it hasn't been vaccinated after all, any treatment at the vet's ought to _____ by the people that sold it."
5. "If people know the facts about puppy trafficking, it's not so likely that they _____ _____ in this way when they start looking for a pet."

to vaccinate ['væksɪneɪt] *impfen*

6 Translation: Expressing ideas without the passive

a) *Look at these German sentences. How can you express the same ideas in English – **without** using the passive?*

1. An Kleidung wird bei Jugendlichen nicht gespart.
   _____

2. Da der Trockner *(tumble dryer)* viel Strom benötigt, sollte auf ihn verzichtet werden.
   _____

3. Am Wochenende wird gefeiert.
   _____

4. Auf der Party wurde viel getanzt und gesungen.
   _____

b) *Now look at these English sentences. Express them in German – **without** using the passive.*

1. King Arthur is said to have been a leader of the Britons.
   _____

2. Tintagel Castle on the Cornish coast is thought to have been his birthplace.
   _____

3. We were followed along the cliff path by a very friendly dog.
   _____

4. I've been given free tickets for 'Camelot'.
   _____

5. Have you been offered the job?
   _____

6 Using indirect speech

A Indirect speech with tense shift

When people talk to each other, they normally use **direct speech.** But if you want to report to another person something that you have heard, you use **indirect speech.**

If the report is given later, the introductory verb is often used in the past tense. In this case the tenses that were used in direct speech have to be changed. The tenses are shifted **one tense further back into the past** (*present → past, present perfect → past perfect* etc.).

If the report is made at a later time or in a different place, **adverbials of time and place** have to be changed: *today → that day; tomorrow/the next day → the following day, yesterday → the day before, five years ago → five years before/previously; here → there.* Also, *this → that.*

Saturday May 23rd   Monday May 25th

Tip
In **modern colloquial English** people tend to use the backshift of tenses less and less: *"I'll have a look at the new stadium tomorrow."* → *Tom said he'll have a look at the new stadium tomorrow.* But when you write texts yourself, using indirect speech, it's best to keep to the traditional rules. You'll avoid making mistakes that way.

Tip
The backshift from *past tense* to *past perfect* is often avoided in favour of the less formal *past tense*: *Mr Johnson mentioned the fact that he first met (had met) the Globo representatives five years ago.*

Tip
In **newspaper articles** the backshift of tenses is often avoided by putting what is reported in quotation marks: *"This arena will become the pride of the whole region."* → *The mayor finished by saying 'This arena will become the pride of the whole region.'*

Basic rules

Direct speech	Backshift of tenses	Indirect speech
Mayor Steve Johnson's speech at the opening ceremony of the 'Globo Arena':		**What the 'Chronicle' reported 2 days later:**
"The opening of the Globo Arena today **is** a truly historic moment."	present tense → past tense	The Mayor said that the opening of the Globo Arena on Saturday **was** a truly historic moment.
"And although it **is raining** <u>here</u> at the moment, in everybody's heart the sun **is shining**."	present progressive → past progressive	He added that although it **was raining** <u>there</u> at the moment, in everybody's heart the sun **was shining**.
"We **have** all **been looking** forward to <u>this</u> great occasion."	present perfect progressive → past perfect progressive	He said that everybody **had been looking forward** to <u>that</u> great occasion.
"It **was** only five years <u>ago</u> that I **met** with the representatives of Globo Communications Systems."	past tense → past perfect	He went on to say that it **had been** only five years <u>previously</u> that he **had met** with the representatives of Globo Communications Systems.
"It is amazing what **has been achieved** since then with the new arena."	present perfect → past perfect	He exclaimed that it was amazing what **had been achieved** since then with the new arena.
"Very soon there **will be** exciting football matches and outstanding pop concerts <u>here</u>."	will → would	Mr Johnson prophesied that very soon there **would be** exciting football matches and outstanding pop concerts <u>there</u>.

Using indirect speech

B Indirect questions and commands

Basic rules

Indirect questions
If there is a question word in direct speech *(When? Why?)* it is used again in indirect speech.
If there is no question word in direct speech, you use *if* or *whether* to introduce the clause in indirect speech.

Direct speech	Indirect speech
'Chronicle' reporter: "**When** was the decision to build the stadium made?" "**Why** didn't you consider a local architect?"	The reporter from the 'Chronicle' wanted to know **when** the decision to build the stadium had been made. She wondered **why** they hadn't considered a local architect.
"**Will** schools be allowed to use the stadium?" "**Did** the Globo people really donate a million pounds to your party?"	She asked the Mayor **if** schools would be allowed to use the stadium. She also enquired **whether** the Globo people had really donated a million pounds to the Mayor's party.

Indirect commands
You can use *tell, advise, ask* and *warn* to introduce indirect commands.
These introductory verbs are followed by a **direct object** and an **infinitive** with *to*.
For negative imperatives, *not + infinitive* with *to* is used.

Direct speech	Indirect speech
"So, my friends, **give** the Globo representatives a big round of applause. And **don't believe** any stories invented by our political opponents."	Mr Johnson **told** everyone **to give** the Globo representatives a big round of applause. And he **warned** them **not to believe** any stories invented by their political opponents.

1 Too many elephants?

In 2008, after 14 years during which the killing of elephants in South Africa was strictly against the law, a new plan to start controlling their numbers was announced. A newspaper reporter spoke to Jon Bouman, a spokesman for the Ministry of Environmental Affairs and Tourism.

Write a newspaper report, using the backshift of tenses where appropriate. You needn't repeat every detail that was mentioned. → A, B

> Q: Is it true that the culling of elephants will soon be reintroduced in South Africa?
> A: We have been reviewing the situation, yes, and have come to the conclusion that elephant numbers will have to be controlled.
> Q: How many elephants will be killed? Animal rights groups have suggested the figures may be anything up to 10,000!
> A: That is absurd. Culling will only be allowed as a last resort.
> Q: What is the reason for this new plan? Are there really too many elephants?
> A: I'm afraid so. Since 1994, the number of elephants in South Africa has risen from about 8,000 to over 20,000. In the Kruger National Park alone, there are about 15,000! That is simply too many.
> Q: What harm do they do?
> A: Wherever they go, they leave behind them a trail of destruction. The fact is, just one elephant eats about 170 kilos of grass, leaves, and bark from trees every day! I agree that it is a terrible thing to have to reduce their numbers by culling, but the Ministry hopes it will only have to be done for a short time, so that in future we can keep the population in check with other measures.
> Q: Is it true that animal rights defenders are threatening to encourage tourists to boycott our national parks if this plan goes ahead?
> A: This may be a possibility, but I can only stress that it is our duty to protect all species, even including plants. Not just elephants. If there is an overpopulation of elephants, it automatically endangers the lives of many other species in the area.

Tip
"A newborn elephant weighs about 100 kilos."
→ *The ranger told us that a newborn elephant weighs/weighed about 100 kilos.*

For facts that do not change (or are accepted as true), the simple present is usually not 'shifted back' when reporting.

Tip
You can start like this:
When asked whether it was true that ..., Jon Bouman explained that ...

Introductory verbs that may be useful:
explain • answer • stress • state • emphasize • argue • point out • admit • make it clear • add

1 to cull to kill (animals) in order to reduce their numbers • **13 as a last resort** after everything else has been tried

Using indirect speech

2 Indirect speech in conversation

Indirect speech is often used quite naturally in conversation, for example if things happen differently from what we expect, if there is some doubt about facts – or if we misunderstand what someone has said …

Use indirect speech to complete these short dialogues, using suitable ideas of your own. → A

Examples: – You'll need your umbrella when you go into town today.
– But **the weather forecast said it would be sunny!**

– I've stopped seeing Julia altogether now.
– What? **I thought she was your best friend!**

> **Tip**
> As you can see from the second example, indirect speech can be used for thoughts as well as for spoken or written words.

1. I'm going to have a very small birthday party this year.
   – But you said _____

2. I saw John in the back row of the cinema with Kate last night.
   – Really? I thought _____

3. Have you heard? The Taplings are moving to Oxford!
   – You've got it wrong! Mrs Tapling told my mother _____
   _____

4. We needn't hand in our English essays till next Monday.
   – Are you sure? I thought Mr Cunningham said _____
   _____

5. It's no good giving Samantha a book. She'll never read it.
   – What? I always thought _____

6. Wait! You needn't rush off to get the last bus. Jonathan will take you home in his car.
   – Oh, is he still here? Great! I thought _____

7. Hurry up, or we'll miss the beginning of the concert. It starts at 7.30, remember.
   – 7.30?! But you told me _____

8. I've decided to go straight to university after I leave school.
   – But the last time we talked about it, you said _____
   _____

9. Poor old Tom. Bad luck he failed his driving test.
   – Failed? But Sally told me _____

10. I'm afraid the book you ordered hasn't come in yet.
    – Oh? Why not? You told me _____
    _____

3 Father and son

Look at the cartoon. Then think of three other things the boy's dad could have said and how the boy reports them to his friend. → A, B

Using indirect speech

4 What they actually said

Imagine what was actually said. → A, B

1. Anna: Diana told me last Friday that she was going to a wedding the following day.

   Diana's actual words: _____

2. Mrs Brown: When I saw Mrs Pearce at the supermarket last week, she said they'd only got back from the USA the evening before!

   Mrs Pearce's actual words: _____

3. Mandy: I got a postcard from John this morning. He said they'd just arrived in Athens – and he said it was incredibly hot there!

   What John wrote: _____

4. Mark: Uncle Andrew wasn't looking too good when I last saw him. He told me he'd had an operation only a few days before.

   Uncle Andrew's actual words: _____

5. Charlie: The police officer asked me whether I knew the woman that had been arrested for shoplifting, and how often she'd come into the shop the week before.

   What the police officer asked: _____
   _____

5 An interview with Daniel Craig

In most situations, instead of giving a word-for-word report of what a person has said, it is normal just to give the 'gist' – in the form of a summary of the main points.
First read what Daniel Craig said in an interview when work on his second James Bond film was completed. Then mark the most important points, and write a summary of the interview. → A, B

You can start like this:
When he was asked how he had felt after finishing filming, Craig said it had been a relief, because they'd been away from home a lot, which he found tiring.

How did it feel to finish filming 'Quantum of Solace'?
A huge relief. In a good way, though. It was much harder because we were away from home for a lot longer – at least half of the six month shoot we were on the road. It was tiring at times, but it was worth it.

Was it more demanding than 'Casino Royale'?
It was really. This one I was involved with months before we started shooting; looking at the script, getting involved with casting, it's been more than just the shooting period. And this time physically there's been a lot more to do.

It was reported that you were injured on set. What happened?
I chopped off the end of my finger and I lost the power in the finger, but it's really healed amazingly. There's a postage stamp scar. I was slamming a door on Mathieu's face so I probably deserved it, ha ha ha! And I got eight stitches in my face from a kick. That was nothing really. I was back at work immediately. It's tiny stuff. But the thing is, it got reported and it always does because there is always a story that leaks out somewhere from set.

There's a spectacular scene where Bond is trapped in a blazing building. What was that like to film?
Exceptional. Our special effects supervisor Chris is a genius. We had a sequence that is at the end of the movie and basically it's the destruction of this building that is blowing up. And I'm in there. I mean, I'm doing stuff, but obviously I have a stunt double at those really kind of dangerous moments. But you have fireballs exploding around you. I'm not kidding, you can feel the heat.

Did you enjoy the travel and the locations?
The locations are fantastic. It's a mindset as much as anything. Colon and Panama City were outstanding places – weird, weird places to be, and very far away from home. But the people were just so friendly and willing and excited about us being there. And being in Chile at 10,000 feet (3,048 metres) up at a space observatory with nobody else around was just amazing. And Italy is a fantastic place. There's a shot coming into Siena, and it's like a piece of animation, it's outrageous.

From: *First News*, 129, October 31, 2008

Using indirect speech

6 Buy it, wear it, chuck it: the price of fast fashion

First, read the text.

Growing demand for cheap clothes is putting an increasing social and environmental strain on the world, a report has said. It questions the sustainability of the 'fast fashion' that is growing in popularity among UK shoppers.

Chains selling bargain outfits have boomed in the past five years, with many fashion followers throwing away garments after one season.

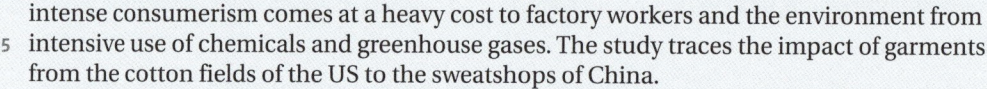

An academic analysis of the global textiles business indicates that such intense consumerism comes at a heavy cost to factory workers and the environment from intensive use of chemicals and greenhouse gases. The study traces the impact of garments from the cotton fields of the US to the sweatshops of China.

The report said UK retailers were increasingly specifying codes of practice for labour standards, but added: "There are difficulties in imposing these codes of practice, and this leads to concerns about working hours, safety and use of child labour."

The throw-away culture was also a problem, the report said. Although the public recycle newspapers and bottles, only one eighth of clothes are recycled through charity shops, the study claimed.

"Waste volumes are high in the UK," it said. "On average UK consumers send 30 kg of clothing and textiles per capita to landfill each year." To illustrate their findings, researchers traced the life cycle of a typical T-shirt.

The raw material comes from the US, where cotton is often grown using pesticides. The yarn is made into clothes in Asia, often by Chinese women working in tough conditions.

Julian Atwood, the lead researcher, said although most in the UK believed recycling glass bottles was good for the environment, they did not realize clothing production uses 10 times more energy than glass.

Regarding Chinese sweatshops, the report said: "The law restricts working hours to eight per day. However, these rules may be overlooked. Working conditions can be hard and some workers may work up to 12-hour shifts, seven days a week."

The Independent, December 1, 2006

5 **sustainability** *here: dauerhafte Umweltverträglichkeit* • 11 **garment** an item of clothing • 17 **retailer** *Einzelhändler* • 17 **code of practice** rules to be followed • 19 **concern** *Sorge* • 24 **per capita** *pro Kopf* • 24 **landfill** *Mülldeponie* • 27 **yarn** *Garn*

a) *Find the three examples in the text in which indirect speech with backshift of tenses is used, and mark them. Write down what the original wording of the report would have been.* → A

_____

_____

_____

_____

b) *Now find the examples of direct speech in the text, and mark them. Then rewrite the sentences, using indirect speech (with backshift of tenses where appropriate).* → A

The report said _____

_____

_____

_____

c) **Mediation:** *Summarise the information from the text in German. Before you start, underline the facts you find most important. Use indirect speech in German wherever it seems appropriate.*

> **Tip**
> Generally speaking, even in 'formal' texts such as newspaper articles, indirect speech is often avoided. Instead, facts are often stated without an 'introductory clause', or direct speech ("…") is used.

Using indirect speech

7 Lev finds work in London

Read this extract from The Road Home *by Rose Tremain, a highly praised novel that describes the experiences of Lev, who comes over to London from his hometown Baryn in the Ukraine, hoping to find work in order to help his family back home.*

With a friend's help, Lev at last finds a job as a kitchen porter in a restaurant kitchen. The afternoon before he starts work, Damian, the restaurant manager, interviews him and shows him the kitchen where he will work.

Lev would start the following day, reporting for work at four.
  "Don't forget, Olev," said Damian, as he walked Lev to the kitchen door, "that a restaurant kitchen operates exactly like an orchestra. Everybody has to focus up and keep time. And there's only one conductor and that's the head chef. So keep alert. Don't rest. Don't take breaks. Keep playing your instrument and play it in time. Then you'll do well. See you tomorrow."

  Lev came out into the sunshine, rolled a cigarette and lit it. On the other side of the street, a few drinkers still occupied a pub table, and their laughter was like the laughter of children, unrestrained and loud. Lev sat down near them and one of the women, a smoker, said flirtatiously, "Hi, Peaches!" and the men turned round to look at Lev, but only for a moment, because their drinks were what they held to and no stranger could part them from their concentration on those.

  Lev ordered a beer. He'd earned this small celebration. He was part of the British economy now. He didn't have to go back to delivering leaflets for Ahmed. He could send another card to Ina, telling her he had a job, paying £5.30 per hour, which was far more than he could earn in Baryn in a day.

  But then he remembered that money had a new terror here.

  The room Lydia had found him in Tufnell Park was going to cost £90 a week. Added to this would be his Tube and bus fares, and his food and his cigarettes. How much would be left to send to Ina? Would anything be left? Lev looked at the young woman who had called him 'Peaches'. How did she manage to live and grow fat and drink away the hours of a Wednesday afternoon? How did she afford it? The woman repelled him: her bulging belly, the greasy skin of her face flaming in the London sun. He preferred to remain alone, sipping the cold beer. He spread out his Underground map and began to plan his journey to Tufnell Park.

From: *Rose Tremain, The Road Home, 2007*

kitchen porter *Küchenhilfe* • 23 **Ina:** Lev's mother • 30 **to repel** [rɪˈpel] *abstoßen*

> **Tip**
> When you read novels and short stories, you will find that authors often use '**inner monologue**'. This is a stylistic device that shows a character's unspoken thoughts and feelings. As with indirect speech, personal pronouns, etc. are changed where necessary, and the tenses are shifted back. But the introductory verb is usually left out, and the word order (e.g. in questions) is just the same as in direct speech.

a) *First identify the parts of the narrative that describe the actions of the characters in this scene from the novel, and mark them in colour. Then, using a different colour, mark the passages of inner monologue (which show the reader what Lev is thinking, feeling, planning and wondering).* → A

b) *Make your own experiments with the style of the text:* → A, B

  1. Turn what Damian says to Lev into indirect speech. Make it 'flow' as well as you can.
     Example: As Damian walked Lev to the kitchen door, he told him …
  2. Try changing the inner monologue, so that the first part of it is expressed as direct speech:
     Example: Lev ordered a beer, thinking to himself, "Well, I've earned this celebration, haven't I? …"
  3. Then express the second part of the inner monologue as indirect speech.
     Example: Lev realised that the room … He knew … He wondered …
  4. Finally compare what you have written with the original text. Discuss which version you think sounds better and why.
  5. Explain why the author has chosen to use inner monologue in so much of this passage from the novel and what effect this has on the reader.

Linking ideas

A Forming complex sentences

You can link different ideas by combining a **main clause** with **subordinate clauses** to form complex sentences.

> Children's football teams have been banned from publishing the results of their league matches because the Football Asscociation believes that it
> 5 puts young people under too much pressure.
> The new rules, which come into force in September and will affect tens of thousands of teams with players
> 10 aged under 8, have caused anger among some parents who believe that young players should be entitled to know how successful they have been.
>
> *The Times*, June 27, 2008

> **Tip**
> '... *banned from publishing*' is a gerund construction.
> For the use of **gerunds** and **participles** to connect sentence parts see **E Gerunds and participles p. 63**.

In the two complex **sentences** above there are two **main clauses** and a number of different **subordinate clauses**:

main clauses	subordinate clauses
Children's football teams have been banned from publishing the result of their league matches ...	**adverbial clause of reason** ... *because the Football Association believes* ... ***that* clause** ... *that it puts young people under too much pressure.*
The new rules ... have caused anger among some parents ...	**relative clause (non-defining)** ..., *which come into force in September and will affect tens of thousands of teams with players aged under 8,* ... **relative clause (defining)** ... *who believe* ... ***that* clause** ... *that young players should be entitled to know* ... **indirect question** ... *how successful they have been.*

> **Tip**
> Sentence parts, clauses and whole sentences can be linked by the conjunctions *and*, *or* and *but*: ... *and will affect tens of thousands* ...

> **Tip**
> '... *players aged under 8*' is an example of a **past participle** used to shorten a relative clause. (see **E Gerunds and participles p. 63**)

- **Just like in German**, **subordinate clauses** can come after the **main clause** or before it:
  As so many children love the game, there are tens of thousands of football teams.
  There are tens of thousands of football teams because so many children love the game.

- **Relative clauses** often appear in the middle of main clauses:
  *The new rules, **which come into force in September,** have annoyed many parents.*

- **Different from German**, the **word order** in any standard affirmative clause is always:

  subject – verb – object :

  English: If you play football , you try to win .

  German: *Wenn man Fußball spielt , versucht man zu gewinnen .*

> **Tip**
> If the subordinate clause comes after the main clause, there is usually no **comma**; if it comes before it, there is normally a comma.

Linking ideas

1 Is there anybody there?

Read the text below and underline all the subordinate clauses. → **A**
Use different colours for: • *relative clauses (green),* • *indirect questions (black),* • *all other subordinate clauses (blue).*

Have you ever wondered whether there is life anywhere else in the universe? Since the universe is so vast, it does indeed seem very probable that there are other planets somewhere out there that are inhabited by intelligent beings of some kind. For a long time scientists who tended to believe this were faced with a paradox: if there really were aliens on other planets,
5 why had none of them ever come to visit the Earth?

Physicists now think they know the answer. Extraterrestrials haven't found us yet because they simply haven't had enough time. A computer simulation of our own galaxy, the Milky Way, has been used to show how a faraway civilisation might send probes into space in search of habitable planets. These probes would have to confine their search to the 'right' parts of the
10 Milky Way, where solar systems are so close to the centre that they have the right elements for the formation of life-sustaining planets. On the other hand, any solar systems that are too close to the centre of the Milky Way would be in constant danger from asteroids or radiation.

Even if alien space ships could travel through space at a speed of 30,000 km a second, which is one tenth of the speed of light, it would take as long as ten billion years to explore only four
15 percent of our galaxy! Even if alien civilisations tried to find us through radio and television broadcasts, it would still be millions of years before they would be able to reach us.

"There are so many stars in the galaxy that probably life could exist elsewhere," says Rasmus Bjork, a Danish researcher. As distances are so incredibly great, however, there is simply no chance that we will be able to get in contact with other colonised planets.

8 **probe** *Raumsonde* • 9 **to confine** to limit • 12 **radiation** *Strahlung*

> **Tip**
> Sometimes *that* clauses begin **without** the word *that*: *It's hard to imagine the Earth is moving.*

> **Tip**
> Clauses with *where* can be seen as relative clauses: *Is this the street where you live?*

B Sentences with adverbial clauses

There are adverbial clauses of time, reason, condition (*if* clauses), etc. These adverbial clauses add extra details to the information that is given in the main clause.
There are a number of typical **conjunctions** that can be used to introduce the different adverbial clauses.

> **Tip**
> Be careful: in an adverbial clauses expressing a **consequence** or **result** there is always a word like *so* or *such* before the word *that*: *It was so wet that we stayed in.*

Basic rules	
Adverbial clauses of time conjunctions: *when, as, after, while, as soon as, before, until/till, since*	*We were cycling along the river* **when it started to rain heavily**. **As soon as the rain had stopped**, *we rode on.* **Just as we were leaving the village**, *the sun came out.*
Adverbial clauses of reason conjunctions: *as/since, because*	**As/Since we hadn't booked any rooms for the night**, *it took us a long time to find a suitable hotel.*
Adverbial clauses of condition conjunctions: *if, even if, unless*	*We won't be able to go on* **unless we can repair the bike.** (See **D Conditional sentences** p. 60 for more details on the use of tenses.)
Adverbial clauses of concession and contrast conjunctions: *although/though/even though* (concession) *while/whereas* (contrast)	**Although he had his bike checked** *before the trip, it kept breaking down.*
Adverbial clauses of comparison conjunctions: *as/like, as if/as though*	*They raced down that hill* **as if they were taking part in the Tour de France**.
Adverbial clauses of purpose and result conjunctions: *so that, so/such … that*	*Let's leave early in the morning* **so that we get to Canterbury in good time**.

(For gerund and participle constructions instead of adverbial clauses see **E Gerunds and participles**.)

> **Tip**
> The conjunction *since* can introduce both an adverbial clause of time or an adverbial clause of reason:
> *I haven't seen them since we went on that bike trip last summer.* (… seit …)
> *Since I haven't got their address, I find it difficult to contact them.* (Da …)

55

Linking ideas

2 Putting it together: The story of Hastings

Decide which sentence parts belong together. → B

The year 1066 was a decisive date in English history.
In the spring of that year the King of England, Edward the Confessor, died, but he left no son to succeed him …

1. Harold, an English nobleman, was chosen by the English as King Edward's successor, although…
2. The King of Norway and William Duke of Normandy both decided to attack, so…
3. The Norwegians landed in the North of England in September, while…
4. At the Battle of Stamford Bridge near York, the English beat the Norwegians so soundly that…
5. Harold and his men were resting at York when…
6. The Normans were able to rest for over a fortnight near Hastings before…
7. Harold's men spent the evening before the battle eating and drinking, whereas…
8. The battle next day, long and bloody, went on until…
9. The English gave up as soon as…

a) they saw their leader dead on the field.
b) the remaining men returned to Norway with only 24 of the 300 ships they had arrived in.
c) two other men also had a claim to the throne.
d) the Normans turned that night into a time of prayer.
e) Harold was finally killed, some say by an arrow in the eye.
f) Harold was actually threatened by two enemies at the same time.
g) William was waiting in France for the right wind to take his ships across the Channel.
h) they received news of Duke William's landing on the south coast.
i) Harold and his army, exhausted after a 10-day march south, finally arrived.

So the battle was lost – and England had been successfully invaded for the last time.

3 Different conjunctions – different meanings

Complete each of the sentences below in two different ways, using the conjunctions to form suitable subordinate clauses. → B

1. I feel great today
   - because _____
   - even though _____

2. We'll be in the Cup Final
   - if _____
   - unless _____

3. It's best not to do strenuous exercise
   - shortly before _____
   - just after _____

4. I'm going to save up for a car
   - so that _____
   - although _____

Linking ideas

4 Using conjunctions to link your ideas

Link the ideas in these bits of spoken English, using conjunctions to make clear, logical sentences. Try to use as many different conjunctions as you can. → A, B

Example: John's sister works at the library. She never seems to read any books.
John's sister works at the library, **but** she never seems to read any books.
or: **Although** John's sister works at the library, she never seems to read any books.
or: John's sister never seems to read any books, **even though** she works at the library.

> but • and • or • as/since • because • when • so • as soon as • even though … • …

1. Our grandparents don't often visit us. They live so far away. _____

2. My father likes watching tennis. He's never actually played himself. _____

3. We've still got some tomatoes left. We could make a soup. They might be nice in a salad.

4. The whistle blew at the end of the match. Crowds of fans ran onto the pitch. _____

5. There's an Italian restaurant on North Street. It's usually fully booked on Saturday evenings. Maybe we won't get a table. _____

6. Jon and Barbie left. It was quite early. We sat down again. We watched a thriller on TV.

C Sentences with relative clauses

Relative clauses are used to give definitions or to add extra information. There are two types of relative clauses: **defining relative clauses** and **non-defining relative clauses**.

Basic rules

Defining relative clauses

Defining relative clauses give necessary information. Without them the meaning of the main clause would be unclear. **Who** and **that** are the relative pronouns used for people. **Which** and **that** are used for things.	*The people **who/that** settled in America first were nomadic tribes from Asia. Some of the large animals **which/that** lived in America at that time have become extinct since then.*
The **relative pronoun** can be left out if it is the object of the relative clause (which then becomes a **contact clause**).	*The tepees **(which/that)** many of the Indian tribes built were made from the skins of animals.*
You can also introduce relative clauses with **whose** + noun. **Whose** expresses a relationship.	*I know a boy **whose** ancestors came to America on the 'Mayflower'. (… dessen Vorfahren …)*

Linking ideas

Basic rules

Non-defining relative clauses

Non-defining relative clauses add extra information. This can make the sentence more interesting. But the main clause is complete and understandable without them. **Who** is used for people, **which** and **whose** are used for things.

A relative clause with **which** can also be used to **comment** on the main clause.

Christopher Columbus, **who came to America in 1492**, arrived about 500 years after the Vikings had discovered the continent.
The Great Plains were the home of the buffalo, **which provided the Sioux Indians with food and clothing**.
Millions of buffalo were killed at the end of the 19th century, **which meant the end of the Native Americans' traditional way of life**.

Tip
Do not use *that* in non-defining relative clauses!

Defining relative clauses	Non-defining relative clauses
No commas: There is **no comma** between main clause and defining relative clause.	**Commas:** There are **commas** – and a pause in speaking – between main clause and relative clause.
Prepositions: In most cases the preposition comes after the verb (+ object). The relative pronoun is often left out (→ contact clause).	**Prepositions:** In non-defining relative clauses, the preposition usually comes before the relative pronoun, but can also come after the verb.
*The Sioux chief **(who/that)** we talked **to** was a descendant of Sitting Bull.* *The small house **(which/that)** he lived **in** was shaped like a tepee.*	*Chief Joseph, **with whom** the American government had negotiated a peace treaty, was later betrayed and driven off his land.* *The Battle of Little Bighorn, **of which** Native Americans are still proud today, was the last Indian victory.*
In **very formal** English the preposition comes before *who/whom/which*; in this case, the relative pronoun cannot be left out.	or: *The Battle of Little Bighorn, **which** Native Americans are still proud **of** today, was the last Indian victory.*
*The tepees **in which** many Native Americans lived were usually made of buffalo skins.* *In the Sioux tradition it was the women **to whom** the tepees belonged.*	

(See **E Gerunds and participles** for participle constructions instead of relative clauses.)

5 Native Americans then and now

Use what you know about the Native Americans to help complete these sentences with suitable relative clauses. Add commas only where they are needed. → C

1. The Sioux Indians depended on the buffalo _____
   _____

2. When Europeans first began to settle in North America, the only people _____
   _____ were Native Americans.

3. Christopher Columbus _____ called these people 'Indians'.

4. Some of the Native Americans _____ have moved to towns and cities,
   but others still try to live according to the traditions _____
   _____

"Is that all there is to life? – buffalo and buffalo by-products?"

6 Creative writing

Look at the cartoon. What might the squaw answer? Write a short dialogue, using relative clauses. → C

Linking ideas

7 The danger of cool rooms in Asia

First read the basic facts as they are presented in the text below. Then, to improve the text and make it more informative, change the extra details in the box into relative clauses that can be added to the text in the right places. Mark these places in the text, then rewrite it so that the relative clauses are incorporated. Finally, read the new text through to check if it sounds good. → C

> Not so very long ago, it was believed that the damaged ozone layer was beginning to recover. This seemed to be good news. But at the end of 2006, scientists discovered that the ozone hole had grown in size again. This is partly because more and more people in the hot parts of the world such as India and southern China are using old-style air conditioners. This fast-growing
> 5 threat to the ozone layer is caused by ordinary city-dwellers. Millions of Asians now have air conditioners in their apartments. Rising standards of living in India and China have made it possible for more and more people to improve the comfort of their homes. It may be some time before developing countries can convert to newer, more ozone-friendly standards.

1 **ozone layer** *Ozonschicht*

> 1. The ozone layer protects the earth from harmful solar rays.
> 2. The ozone hole was first created mostly by gases in aerosol sprays, old refrigerators and old air conditioners.
> 3. Old-style air conditioners have been banned in Europe for some time.
> 4. In hot Asian cities, many people's incomes have improved, and these people simply want cooler homes.
> 5. Ten or fifteen years ago, most Asians would have considered air conditioners to be an unnecessary luxury.
> 6. India and China are the most populous countries in the world.
> 7. In developing countries, the use of ozone-depleting chemicals is still officially allowed.

8 Living with a couple and sharing the rent

First read what Robert, Sally and William say about their living arrangements.

> *Robert, 26:* Last year I moved into a flat in Islington, North London. I share it with a young couple, Sally and William. Sally is a friend. I met her at Warwick University several years ago. The monthly rent would be too high for Sally and William on their own. We all three share the cost of the rent.
> 5 *Sally, 27:* The system works very well, but in a way it's a strange idea. Not everybody would be keen on it! But Robert keeps very regular hours, and does a lot of the housework. He's an ideal lodger!
> *William, 28:* The alternative would have been to live with a total stranger in the flat. Neither Sally nor I wanted to do that. Now that Robert pays a third of the rent, we can do lots of
> 10 things – like having foreign holidays. We couldn't afford things like that otherwise.
> *Robert:* The atmosphere is very homely and relaxed. I feel that's important! And I've never felt I was in the way. That's really something! I appreciate it more than words can say.

7 **lodger** ['lɒdʒə] *Untermieter*

Now write a text describing the situation, and linking ideas with relative clauses where you can. → C

- Last year Robert moved into a flat in Islington, North London, which he shares …
- According to Sally, the system …
- As William explains, …
- For Robert, the atmosphere …

Linking ideas

9 Expressing ideas less formally

There are many situations, especially in the context of everyday spoken English, when relative clauses beginning with prepositions sound much too formal. The sentences below are examples. Make them sound better – and more natural – by using contact clauses with the preposition after the verb. → C

1. Could you tell me the name of the book club to which you belong?
   _____

2. Who was the person to whom you were talking on the bus yesterday?
   _____

3. Riding my bike in city traffic is a thing of which I've always been rather frightened!
   _____

4. Jamie has been offered that job for which he applied last month.
   _____

5. Emma is that cousin about whom I've told you so often.
   _____

6. This is a holiday to which I've been looking forward a lot.
   _____

7. The parcel for which you've been waiting has arrived.
   _____

8. The boy with whom my sister has started going out now is called Patrick.
   _____

9. What was it about which we were just talking?
   _____

10. Mr Carter said exercise 6 was the one on which we should spend most time.
    _____

D Conditional sentences

Tip
Don't use the *will* future, the conditional or the conditional perfect in *if*-clauses.

Conditional sentences consist of an *if* **clause** and a **main clause**. The *if* clause expresses a **condition** and the main clause describes the **consequence**.
Although many combinations of tenses are possible in conditional sentences, it may help you if you concentrate on three basic types.

Basic rules

Type 1 **Realistic condition** The condition may be fulfilled.	*If* clause: **simple present** main clause: **will** future	If Pamela **gets** the job with the BBC, she **will move** to London.
Type 2 **Theoretical condition** The condition is unlikely to be fulfilled or is purely theoretical.	*If* clause: **simple past** main clause: **conditional**	Ben **would have** a better chance of a job in Switzerland if he **spoke** French and German.
Type 3 **Condition no longer possible** The condition can no longer be fulfilled because it refers to a past situation which is over now.	*If* clause: **past perfect** main clause: **conditional perfect**	If your mother **had applied** for it, she **would** probably **have been offered** the position of headmistress.

Linking ideas

Other frequently used combinations of tenses in conditional sentences

simple present If you really **want** the job,	modal auxiliary you **must** try to create a good impression at the interview.
	imperative **don't forget** to apply for it in good time.
If you **write** 'Dear Sirs',	simple present it **sounds** much better than 'Hi Guys'.
past perfect If Tom **had accepted** the job in Los Angeles,	conditional he **would be earning** a lot of money now.
subjunctive If I **were** you,	conditional I**'d send** the manager an e-mail straight away.

10 Different forms for different situations

Decide, according to each situation, which type of conditional is suitable. → D

1. I haven't asked Mum about the car yet. I _____ (collect) you at seven if she _____ (let) me have it. I _____ (let) you know in time if she _____ (say) no.

2. I wonder why Lucy wasn't at the party last night. I'm sure she _____ (come) if she _____ (have) time.

3. Jon says he's gone and lost that book he borrowed! If I _____ (know) he was so careless with other people's things, I _____ (never – lend) it to him.

4. It's awful the way Jenny bosses Adam around! I don't know how he stands it! If she _____ (treat) me like that, I _____ (not go) out with her any more.

5. Watch those pizzas! If you _____ (leave) them in the oven much longer, they _____ (go) dry.

6. Hasn't Susie given you anything towards the cost of the petrol yet? If I _____ (be) you, I _____ (ask) her to pay her share. Maybe she just forgot. I expect she _____ (give) you the money by now if she _____ (think) of it.

7. I'm terribly allergic to cats! Even if someone _____ (show) me a photo of a cat, I _____ (start) sneezing straight away! If I _____ (know) you had this cat, I _____ (never – come) round here for tea today!

Linking ideas

11 A chapter of accidents (a true story)

It happened in Australia in the year 2001. One evening, a man was driving along somewhere south of Brisbane when he ran out of petrol. He got out of the car and fetched the spare can, which he kept filled in case of emergency, out of the boot.

5   He opened the can, absent-mindedly forgetting the fact that he was smoking a cigarette at the time. While he was filling up the tank, the burning cigarette fell into the petrol, causing a sudden explosion.

Not surprisingly, the man was badly burnt. But that was not all. 10 The force of the explosion was so great that he fell backwards and landed on top of an anthill. Feeling in need of a drink to calm him down after all these misfortunes, the man stopped at the next bar he came to and went in.

An hour or so later, when he continued his journey, he was so badly affected by alcohol that he was stopped by the police. The fact that he had no driving licence was then discovered. He was arrested for drink driving and driving without a licence.

11 **anthill** ['ænthɪl] *Ameisenhaufen*

Look carefully at the description of events in the text above, noticing how one thing led to another. Then write at least five sentences with if, *to show the connections between cause and effect.* → D

Example: If the man **had gone** to a filling station in time, he **wouldn't have run** out of petrol.

12 Error spotting

Spot the mistakes. In each of the conditional sentences below, one of the verb forms is wrong. Cross out the wrong forms and correct them. → D

1. It's good we got up so early. If we would have left home later, we would probably have missed our flight. _____

2. We'd better be careful! If we don't remember exactly which storey we parked the car on, we can't find it again later. _____

3. I'll give you my spare car key. It'll be useful if for any reason I ~~lost~~ mine. _____

4. I'm afraid your bag's a bit too big. If it was smaller, you were able to take it on the plane with you as hand luggage. _____

5. We've been lucky with the weather! If the fog didn't lift, our flight might have been delayed for hours. _____

6. Perhaps we ought to listen to the safety instructions. I don't think I had known what to do if we had to make an emergency landing. _____

7. We needn't carry all this luggage. If you wait here, I fetch a trolley. _____

8. A taxi? Are you mad? It'd be far cheaper if we'd go into London by underground. _____

Linking ideas

E Linking sentence parts with gerunds and participles

Basic rules

Gerund constructions

Alternative to subordinate clauses
A gerund construction after **before, on, for, after** and **in spite of** corresponds to a subordinate clause (*After crashing ... = After he (had) crashed ...*). (**See B Sentences with adverbial clauses p. 55**)

After crashing his sports car at 150 mph, James Bond barely escaped with his life.
In spite of suffering serious injuries, James always gets the villains (and the beautiful girl) in the end.

No corresponding subordinate clauses
A gerund is also used after **instead of, by, without, apart from, as well as, what about?, it's worth** and **it's no use**.
There are no adverbial clauses that correspond to these gerund constructions.

Bond escapes from the most difficult situations **by using** a number of high-tech gadgets.
Without thinking about his own life, James saves the world again.
It's **worth going** to the cinema or **buying** the DVD just to see the car chases.

-ing form with a subject of its own
It is possible to put a noun (*people*) or a pronoun (*him*) between the verb and the *-ing* form. This gives the *-ing* form a 'subject of its own'. In these constructions the *-ing* form can be looked upon as a **gerund** or as a **participle**.

I hate **people smoking** in my room.
Mrs Kay doesn't mind **Bruce using** her car.
But she's worried about **him driving** too fast.

Participle constructions

Participle constructions instead of adverbial clauses
These participle constructions correspond to adverbial clauses. (**See B Sentences with adverbial clauses p. 55.**)
They can also be introduced by a conjunction (*while, when, though, as if*).
Participle constructions tend to sound **more formal** than adverbial clauses and are mainly used in written English (e.g. in newspaper reports).

Sweeping through Britain during the night, the extreme weather left a trail of destruction. (**When** it swept through Britain ...)
Warned about heavy rain and violent storms, most people stayed indoors. (**As/Because** they had been warned ...)
A man drowned **while swimming** in heavy seas at Perranporth, Cornwall.

Accompanying circumstances
You can also use participle constructions to describe things that happen at the same time as what is described in the main clause: The participle construction expresses accompanying circumstances.

In Wales several rivers burst their banks, *causing extreme flooding*.
Torrential rain continued to fall, **putting hundreds of homes at risk**.

Tip
There is also a **passive** form of the **gerund**:
Apart from being chased round the world by a gang of ruthless killers, Bond also has to face the advances of Miss Moneypenny...

Tip
In these participle constructions the **present participle** corresponds to **active** verb forms and the **past participle** corresponds to **passive** verb forms:
swimming = he was swimming; *warned* = they had been/were warned.

Tip
There are also other forms of the **participle**:
- the **passive** form:
The car skidded off the road while being overtaken by the police.
- the **perfect** form:
Having called an ambulance, we waited for help to arrive.

Linking ideas

> **Basic rules**
>
> **Participle with a subject of its own**
> These 'absolute' participle constructions have their own subject *(some of the country)*, which is different from the subject of the main clause *(The past 48 hours)*. Participle constructions of this kind sound very formal. When they are introduced by *with*, they sound less formal and can also be used in colloquial English.
>
> *The past 48 hours have been the wettest on record in Wales, **some of the country getting** a month's rainfall in a day.*
> ***With so much rain falling** during the last two days, the ground is so wet that it can't absorb any more.*
> *It's been a busy day for the emergency services, **with dozens of people trapped** in their cars.*
>
> **Participle constructions instead of relative clauses**
> Participle constructions can be used to shorten relative clauses. **(See C Sentences with relative clauses p. 57)**
>
> *Several men **working** on a building site were hurt when a wall collapsed.*
> **(working = who were working)**
> *The workmen **injured** in the accident were airlifted to hospitals in Exeter.*
> **(injured = who were injured)**

13 Expressing things more fluently

Read what the people say. Then think how you could link their ideas by using gerund or participle constructions. → E

Example: You looked after the Browns' dog. Did they pay you anything?
– Did the Browns pay you anything for looking after their dog?

1. He just took the money out of my purse. He didn't ask.

   _____

2. I'm not going to phone Jamie. I've decided to send him an e-mail instead.

   _____

3. Do you know those girls? The ones that are sitting over there by the window?

   _____

4. You helped me so much. Thank you!

   _____

5. We can't just get up and leave. We haven't said goodbye to Paul and Judy.

   _____
   _____

6. Those potatoes that were left over from lunch – have you thrown them away?

   _____

7. You can save a bit of time on the way back. Just take the short cut over the moors.

   _____
   _____

8. I'm a bit worried. My parents may complain if I get back late.

   _____

9. Don't laugh at me. I hate it when people do that!

   _____

10. I couldn't see my way to the bathroom last night. All the lights in the corridor were switched off.

    _____
    _____

Linking ideas

14 The slowly sinking islands of the Torres Strait

a) *Complete the text with suitable gerunds and participles. Read each section before you choose suitable verbs.* → E

disappear • call • have • rise • live

With the sea slowly _____ higher year by year, the islands of the Torres Strait may only survive for a few more years before _____ altogether. The people _____ on the islands, which lie somewhere between the northeastern tip of Australia and Papua New Guinea, are actually Australians, native people officially _____ the 'Torres Strait islanders'. They are a different race from the Aborigines, _____ more in common, ethnically, with the people of Papua New Guinea.

roll • do • wash • destroy • sweep

In recent years unusually high tides, with enormous waves _____ up the beaches and _____ away a lot of the sand, have flooded houses, gardens and roads. The damage _____ by these tides has been shocking, in places with sea walls _____ away into the sea and more and more people's homes _____ .

sea wall Deich

ask • shine • build (2x) • own • fly • surround

Eighteen of the islands are inhabited, but six of them are so flat that there is no higher ground to retreat to. _____ over these low-lying islands in a plane or helicopter, you see them below as little patches of green _____ in the brilliant blue of the ocean _____ them. But even on the rockier islands, the people are used to living near the sea, with most of their houses _____ near the beach where the boats _____ by the local fishermen are moored. _____ whether they might consider solving the problem (at least for a while) by _____ new homes on higher ground, most of the people reply that it would be hard.

to moor to fasten a boat to the land or bottom of the sea, using ropes or an anchor

melt • surround • live • move • hear • rise • threaten

"I simply can't imagine waking up in the mornings," said one islander, "without _____ the sound of the waves." For those _____ on the flatter islands, of course, a move to higher ground is not possible. Meanwhile, reports in the news of huge icebergs _____ and the level of the sea _____ continue to worry the Torres Strait islanders. One thing is certain: life on these small islands _____ by ocean – and _____ by higher and higher tides – is not going to get any easier.

Linking ideas

15 One in four body piercings goes wrong

a) *While you read this newspaper article, mark all the <u>participle</u> and <u>gerund</u> constructions used to link sentence parts.* → E

For many young people, piercings of all parts of the body, hung with jewellery, have become an essential fashion accessory. But they carry significant risks, according to the first survey to examine the complications arising from body art.

One in 10 adults in England has had a piercing somewhere other than the ear lobe, of whom 28 per cent experienced complications and one in 100 was admitted to hospital.

The survey of 10,000 people over 16 in England found nearly 1,000 had a piercing, which was three times more common in women than men. Piercings were most common in the youngest age group, those aged 16 to 24, who were also most likely to suffer complications. Swelling, infection and bleeding were frequent side effects, with tongue piercings the most risky.

Serious complications resulting in hospital admission mostly occurred with piercings performed by non-specialists rather than with those carried out in a tattoo parlour or a specialist piercing shop.

The study was published in the British Medical Journal. One of the researchers said: "It is vital that anyone considering a piercing ensures that they go to a reputable piercer to reduce the possibility of having problems. Your piercer should tell you how to look after the piercing afterwards, and this is important to reduce the likelihood of infections."

The growing popularity of lip and tongue piercings – the most risky – in the youngest age group suggests that "people may be becoming more adventurous", the researchers say. Half of tongue piercings result in complications – usually swelling – and a quarter lead to professional help being sought.

From: *The Independent*, June 13, 2008

29 **reputable** [ˈrepjʊtəbl] known to be good and reliable

b) *Now answer these questions – but where possible **without** using participle or gerund constructions.* → E

1. What did the researchers conducting the study want to find out?
   _____
   _____

2. Which group of people in the survey most often had trouble after their piercings were done?
   _____
   _____

3. Which people were most likely to have to go to hospital as a result?
   _____
   _____

4. What advice was given by one of the researchers?
   _____
   _____

5. What may happen if you have a lip or tongue piercing done?
   _____
   _____

c) *What is your opinion on body art, e.g. piercings and tattoos? Is it worth the risk? Write a short paragraph on the subject, using participle and gerund constructions where appropriate.* → E

Linking ideas

16 One day in court

a) Read the following newspaper article carefully, looking out for examples of:
– adverbial clauses – relative clauses – gerund and participles constructions.
Mark them in three different colours. → A, B, C, E

> **Tip**
> Divide the text up and work in groups for this task.

The scale of youth binge drinking was exposed yesterday in just one youth court where a dozen teenagers claimed that their separate crimes were all alcohol-related.

All 12 youngsters had been arrested after heavy drinking sessions.

Magistrates at Hastings Youth Court, East Sussex, heard that one 15-year-old girl admitted causing affray after drinking 11 bottles of alcopop.

CCTV footage showed her remove one of her knee-high boots and beat a stranger over the head, starting a late-night mêlée in the town centre involving 20 other drunken teenagers.

She could have been sent to youth custody but was instead given 20 hours' community service and ordered to pay £20 costs at £2 per week.

In another case, a 16-year-old youth was caught driving his father's van after consuming cans of strong lager with friends. The level of alcohol in his blood was nearly twice the drink-drive limit when police stopped him.

Another 16-year-old youth who had been drinking cans of strong lager and a two-litre bottle of cider at a park in Rye attacked a fellow teenager for looking at him. His victim suffered a broken nose and such severe facial swelling that he was unable to open his eye.

In another case, a 17-year-old drank lager and cider before rampaging through a housing estate, smashing fences, throwing eggs at windows, swearing at neighbours and spitting in one man's face.

The youth, who admitted criminal damage and assault, was ordered to pay £250 compensation and £100 costs at £5 a week.

Last month it was revealed that the number of teenagers and children convicted of violent crimes had increased from 17,590 to 24,102 a year since 2005.

A study by the Office for National Statistics revealed that thousands of children as young as 12 were drinking regularly "to get drunk". 23 per cent of under-16s said that they had been in trouble with the police after drinking, and 42 per cent said that they started drinking before turning 13.

From: *The Times*, February 26, 2008

---

1 **scale** [skeɪl] *Umfang/Ausmaß* • 1 **binge drinking** [ˈbɪndʒ ˌdrɪŋkɪŋ] drinking too much in a short period of time • 7 **magistrate** [ˈmædʒɪstreɪt] sb who works as a judge in a local court • 9 **affray** [əˈfreɪ] a noisy fight in a public place • 13 **mêlée** [ˈmeleɪ] situation in which a lot of people rush around in confusion • 17 **custody** [ˈkʌstədi] *Haft* • 18 **community service** work (unpaid) that is done to help other people (e.g. as punishment for a crime) • 40 **compensation** [ˌkɒmpənˈseɪʃn] *Entschädigung, Schadensersatz* • 44 **to convict** [kənˈvɪkt] *verurteilen*

Linking ideas

b) *Express the same meaning in a different way..* → A, B, C, E

Example: One 15-year-old girl admitted causing affray. *(Rephrase, using an adverbial clause.)*
– One 15 year-old-girl admitted that she had caused affray.

1. a mêlée in the town centre *involving 20 other drunken teenagers. (Rephrase, using a relative clause.)* _____

2. She *could have been sent to youth custody but was instead given* 20 hours' community service. *(Rephrase, using a gerund construction.)* _____

3. A 16-year-old youth was caught *driving his father's van after consuming cans of strong lager. (Rephrase, using two adverbial clauses.)* _____

4. Another … youth … attacked a fellow teenager *for looking at him. (Rephrase, using an adverbial clause.)* _____

5. A 17-year-old drank lager and cider *before rampaging through a housing estate, smashing fences, throwing eggs at windows, swearing at neighbours and spitting in one man's face. (Rephrase, using an adverbial clause.)* _____

6. The youth, *who admitted criminal damage,* was ordered to pay compensation. *(Rephrase, using a participle construction.)* _____

7. The number of teenagers and children *convicted of violent crimes* had increased. *(Rephrase, using a relative clause.)* _____

17 Europeans come to the continent in the Pacific

Read the facts on the next page. Then use them as the basis for a text of your own. Connect the ideas as logically as you can, to produce a text that is interesting to read. To help your text to 'flow' well, make use of relative clauses, adverbial clauses (introduced by conjunctions such as when, after, although, because, *etc.), and suitable participle or gerund constructions..* → A, B, C, E

When you have finished your text, check it through for mistakes, then read it aloud to see how it sounds. (Compare it with a partner's, too. Then perhaps you can help to improve each other's texts!)

The landing of Captain Cook at Botany Bay, 1770

A portrait of James Cook

1565: A Spanish monk made the first crossing of the Pacific. He was called Andres de Urdaneta. He told exciting stories of the journey. This made people wonder: did a great southern continent lie somewhere west of the tip of South America?

1606: A Dutch captain reached the north coast of a new land. His name was Willem Jantszoon. He was from Amsterdam. This land is what we now know as Australia. The Dutch called it New Holland.

1642: The explorer Abel Tasman (also Dutch) landed on an island further south. It was later called Tasmania.

But the Dutch quickly lost interest in this new continent. They did not settle. Over a hundred years passed.

1770: Captain James Cook landed on the east coast of Australia. He claimed the continent for England. Cook was born in Yorkshire, England. He was a highly intelligent man with a strong character. He was also a gifted navigator and astronomer.

18th century: On average, 60 % of all seamen died on long voyages. 50 % of them died from disease. Cook tried to reduce illness: he introduced strict rules on his first ship, *The Endeavour*. The men had to bathe every day. Their clothes and bed clothes were aired every few days. The ship was fumigated regularly. Cook knew the importance of fresh food. He took plenty of fresh fruit on board. This was to prevent scurvy. Scurvy is a terrible disease. It is caused by a lack of vitamin C. It used to be a common cause of death on ships. Cook also gave his men fresh meat and vegetables as often as possible. This helped to improve their health considerably.

It was Cook who had claimed Australia for England. But the first European settlers didn't arrive until eighteen years later. Most of these settlers were convicts. They were sent to the new continent for this reason: the prisons in Britain had become overcrowded. The convicts helped to build and establish the first colony. It later developed into the city of Sydney.

19th century: More and more colonies were established in Australia. They soon gained self-government. At first they were independent of each other: each had its own parliament and laws.

1901: This changed. The separate colonies all joined together in a federation of states. They called this federation the Commonwealth of Australia.

1 **monk** *Mönch* • 28 **to bathe** [beɪð] to wash yourself in a bath • 30 **to fumigate** to use smoke to remove disease • 33 **scurvy** *Skorbut*

18 What's that in German?

A number of the constructions dealt with in this chapter have no exact equivalent in German. Bearing this in mind, try to find the best way to translate the following sentences. → B, C, E

1. Motivated by their wish to protect the environment, many British families have now decided to spend their holidays nearer home instead of flying to destinations abroad.
2. With the cost of train travel rising and cheap flights getting more and more popular over the years, aviation has become by far the fastest growing source of carbon dioxide in the UK.
3. Between 1990 and 2008, emissions from UK aviation increased by 70 %, with a further doubling of growth expected within the next 20–25 years.
4. The government, though committed to cutting UK carbon dioxide emissions by 60 % between 1990 and 2050, now has to face the fact that this will be impossible if aviation is allowed to keep on expanding.
5. Aviation, now recognised as the most highly polluting form of transport on earth, could be responsible for up to 50 % of the UK's total emissions by 2050, cancelling out any savings by other industries or by individuals.
6. Wanting to counteract this trend, lots of people now prefer to go on driving holidays.
7. According to research published recently, quite a number of others have even cancelled their holidays altogether.
8. It seems increasingly likely that holidays in places like the Lake District, the Scottish Highlands, Wales, Devon or Cornwall will be the ones British families will look forward to in the future.

aviation air travel • **to be committed to doing sth** *sich verpflichten, etw. zu tun*

8 Describing

A Adjectives and adverbs

> **Tip**
> There are a few **adjectives ending in -ly** (e.g. *friendly, lovely*) that don't have adverb forms. Different wording has to be used:
> *She spoke to me in a very friendly way.*

You can use both <u>adjectives</u> and <u>adverbs</u> to **describe people, objects and events.** They can make texts more interesting, more informative and more lively.

> <u>Now</u>, as it turned out, the Rebellion was achieved <u>much earlier</u> and <u>more easily</u> than anyone had expected. In <u>past</u> years Mr. Jones, although a <u>hard</u> master, had been a <u>capable</u> farmer, but <u>of late</u> he had fallen on evil days. He had become <u>much</u> <u>disheartened</u> after losing money in a lawsuit, and had taken to drinking <u>more</u> than was good for him. For <u>whole</u> days at a
> 5 time he would lounge in his Windsor chair in the kitchen, reading the newspapers, drinking, and <u>occasionally</u> feeding Moses on crusts of bread soaked in beer. His men were <u>idle</u> and <u>dishonest</u>, the fields were <u>full</u> of weeds, the buildings wanted roofing, the hedges were <u>neglected</u>, and the animals were <u>underfed</u>.
>
> From: George Orwell, *Animal Farm*, 1945

3 **of late** *(formal)*: recently

> **Tip**
> Verbs that express a state or a quality are followed by an **adjective** – not an adverb. (e.g. *be, become, seem, feel, keep, look* (aussehen), *smell, taste, sound.*)
> <u>Compare:</u>
> *She looked at him **critically**.*
> *She looks **nice** in that blue dress.*

Basic rules

Adjectives describe what someone or something is like. They can be used **attributively** or **predicatively**.	*… a **hard** master, a **capable** farmer, …* → (**attributive** use) *His men were **idle**. The hedges were **neglected**.* → (**predicative** use)
Adverbs describe the way something happens or is done. They can **modify verbs** (*feeding*), adjectives (*disheartened*) and other **adverbs** (*easily*).	*… the Rebellion was achieved … **easily** …* *… **occasionally** feeding …* *… **much** disheartened …* *… **more** easily …*
Adverbs like *obviously, unfortunately, of course* etc. can **comment on a whole sentence**.	***Obviously**, the animals have had enough of Mr. Jones' mismanagement of the farm.*

B Special cases

> **Tip**
> Remember these irregular comparative and superlative forms:
> *good/well:* **better – best**
> *bad/badly:* **worse – worst**
> *many:* **more – most**
> *much:* **more – most**
> *little:* **less – least**

There are some adjectives and corresponding adverbs that can be difficult for Germans to use.

Adverbs that have the same form as adjectives

adjective	adverb
*Zak has got a very **fast** car.* *It was a **long** trip from Chicago to San Diego.* *We took an **early** flight back home.*	*But on American roads he isn't allowed to drive **fast**.* *It didn't take us **long** to reach Cedar Rapids.* *We left our hotel **early** in the morning.*

Further examples of adverbs that have the same form as adjectives:
late, low, far, daily, weekly, monthly.

Adverbs with two different forms

adverb without *-ly*	adverb with *-ly*
*The team have worked very **hard** in the last few weeks.* (**hart/schwer**)	*They can **hardly** wait for the new season to start.* (**kaum**).
*We always try to play **fair**.* (**fair**)	*The title race last season was **fairly** close.* (**ziemlich**)
*Liverpool have **just** scored their second goal.* (**gerade**)	*I don't think the decision to send the player off the field was **justly** made.* (**zu Recht**)
*Cole wanted to tackle Lee, but couldn't get **near** enough.* (**nah**)	*The match is **nearly** over.* (**fast**)
*The match started **late**.* (**spät**)	*We haven't won many games **lately**.* (**in letzter Zeit**)

Describing

1 Recognising adverbs

a) *Look carefully at the words in the box. Underline the adverbs.*
   Mark (in colour) the words you find that can be used both as adverbs and as adjectives. → A, B

> accidentally – actually – apply – assembly – bitter – brilliantly – butterfly – carefully – deadly – definitely – early – easily – extremely – fast – fatally – folly – fortunately – frankly – friendly – gradually – hard – hardly – heavenly – late – lately – lovely – monthly – nervously – obviously – often – particularly – perfectly – pretty – probably – quickly – quiet – quite – recently – simply – suddenly – tragically – ugly – unexpectedly – usually – well – wide

b) *Find the adverbs in these sentences and mark them. Then replace them by adverbs – with the same meaning – from the box.*

1. Luckily, we managed to get home before the rain started. _____
2. The traffic in our neighbourhood is slowly getting worse. _____
3. I enjoy cycling to work, especially when it's warm and sunny. _____
4. We'll certainly go by train if this snowy weather continues. _____
5. It's generally best to avoid driving into the city on a Saturday. _____

c) *Now choose suitable adverbs from the box to complete these sentences. (There may be more than one way to do this.)*

1. Sam played _____ on Saturday and won the tournament _____. Of course, he has worked very _____ on his game _____.
2. It was _____ annoying. We arrived at the concert hall a few minutes _____, and they wouldn't let us into the auditorium. _____, it was our own fault!
3. My grandfather _____ turns up at our house _____. _____, I think he _____ enjoys giving us all a surprise!
4. It's _____ clear. The accident happened _____ because she was driving too _____. _____, two of the people in the other car were _____ injured, and died in hospital.

2 Fancy a farmer?

Decide which form – adjective or adverb – is correct. Where there is an asterisk (*) you need a comparative or superlative form. → A, B

It is _____ (good) known that Wales is an _____ (exceptional) _____ (beautiful) country, with some of the _____ (spectacular*) scenery in the UK. It may sound _____ (ideal) as a place to live. But many _____ (young) farmers in Wales have a problem that is _____ (extreme) _____ (hard) to solve: they _____ (simple) can't find a partner.

The _____ (sad) truth about the countryside today is that it can _____ (actual) be a very _____ (lonely) place. A _____ (high) percentage of people who grow

Describing

up in the countryside _____ (eventual) have to move to cities where they are _____ (likely*) to get a job. _____ (unfortunate) this means that _____ (isolated) farmers find it _____ (difficult), if not _____ (impossible), to meet anyone _____ (new). An _____ (additional) problem is that the _____ (antisocial) hours _____ (general) associated with farming – getting up _____ (early) every day to milk the cows, for example – do not _____ (necessary) attract _____ (potential) partners!

_____ (recent) farmers in Wales hit on an idea that – _____ (hopeful) – may solve the problem, at least for some of them. As a _____ (special) way of celebrating St Dwynwen's Day on 25th January, which is _____ (actual) the Welsh equivalent of St Valentine's Day, they stuck photos of themselves on the side of thousands of milk cartons. On the stickers it _____ (just) says: "Fancy a farmer?" People who feel _____ (interested) can _____ (easy) get in touch with _____ (lonely) farmers via an online dating agency whose address is given on the carton.

Iwan Jones, 30, who spent _____ (near) two hours at the dairy sticking pictures of himself onto cartons, said, "I'm at an age when _____ (many*) people _____ (usual) think about settling down. Unless farmers like me can find wives, we might not have children to carry on our business. I have no _____ (definite) ideas about what I'm looking for in a partner. I _____ (real) can't afford to be _____ (choosy)! In any case, the others are all _____ (good*) looking than me, so I'll _____ (probable) be the last carton left on the shelf!"

to settle down: to get married and start a family • **on the shelf:** unmarried, without a partner

3 Creative writing

a) *Think of another adverb or adverbial phrase that could be used instead of "actually" in this cartoon:* → A

_____

b) *First describe the cartoon. Then write the story behind it, using descriptive adjectives and adverbs wherever suitable (ca. 100 words). Here are some words that might be of help to you:* → A, B

> Buckingham Palace • corgi • press • tabloid • sensational reporter • journalist • to inform • the public • to investigate • in disguise • to be disguised as … • servant • to recognise • competition • to mistake sb for sb else • to be deceived • success

"Actually I'm not the queen – I'm undercover for the Daily Mirror…"

Describing

C The position of adverbs and adverbials in the sentence

Basically there are three positions in the sentence where adverbs and adverbials can be placed:

- before the subject (**front position**),
- between subject and main verb or between auxiliary and main verb (**mid position**),
- after the verb or after verb + object (**end position**).

Which position you decide on depends on the type of adverb or adverbial and the emphasis you want to give it.

Basic rules

Front position

Adverbs of comment (*apparently, basically, frankly, unfortunately, obviously, of course,* etc.) usually appear in front position.

Of course, America has always been a land of immigrants.
Unfortunately, some immigrant groups had to face religious and racial prejudice.

Adverbs and **adverbials of time and place** can appear in front position for emphasis.

By 1860 the original 13 states had more than doubled in number.
In the east urban growth continued rapidly.

Mid position

Adverbs of frequency (*always, often, occasionally, never* etc.) often take mid position.

*New arrivals did not **always** receive a warm welcome.*
*They were **often** scorned by people who had come only a few years before them.*

Adverbs of manner (*easily, quickly, firmly, gradually* etc.) can take mid position.

*Immigrants **firmly** believed that after the initial hardships life would **gradually** become easier.*

End position

Adverbs of manner (*slowly, carefully* etc.) usually appear in end position (after the verb or after verb + object).
When these adverbs appear in end position, they are usually **more strongly emphasised** than in mid position. Very emphatic adverbs like *hard* and *well* always appear in end position.

*The wagon trains moving west could only travel **slowly**.*
*The settler built his house **carefully**.*

*People setting up as farmers had to work **hard**.*

Adverbs and adverbials of place and time (*here, in the Midwest, yesterday, two years ago*) mostly take end position.

*Many German immigrants settled **in the Midwest**.*
*There was an enormous wave of newcomers **at the end of the 19th century**.*

If there are **two adverbials** at the end of a sentence, the normal word order is place before time.

*The government set up an immigration center **on Ellis Island** **in 1892**.*
*Thousands of Germans migrated **to Pennsylvania** **in the 1860s**.*

> **Tip**
> If the main verb in the sentence is *be*, the adverb normally goes after it.
> Compare:
> She **always** arrived late.
> She **was always** late.

> **Tip**
> Different from German:
> Adverbs of manner never go between the verb and the direct object:
> They **quickly** found new jobs.
> Sie **fanden schnell neue Arbeitsplätze**.

> **Tip**
> Adverbs of degree appear before the word they qualify:
> Many immigrants had to face **extremely difficult** conditions.
> Some of them **only** wanted to get rich quickly.

Describing

Tip
The **more exact** time usually comes **before** the **more general** time: *We left at seven o'clock in the evening.*

4 At the seaside

Decide on the best place for the adverbs and adverbials in these sentences. → C

1. Will you come with us? (this afternoon/to the beach)
   _____

2. There are fewer people. (at this end of the beach/usually)
   _____

3. I should have bought that cheap surfboard. (never/frankly)
   _____

4. I'll get us some ice creams. (over there/quickly/at the beach café)
   _____

5. Before Sam went in, he tested the temperature of the water. (actually/with his toe/carefully)
   _____
   _____

6. We had a great holiday. (absolutely/last year/in Cornwall). The weather was good.
   (all the time we were there/luckily/really)
   _____
   _____

7. Max goes for a swim. (before breakfast/sometimes/in the sea)
   _____

8. That nice family hotel closed down. (on the seafront/a few months ago/unfortunately)
   _____

9. The tide comes in. (always/over this flat sandy beach/fast/incredibly)
   _____

10. It'll be high tide. (at 10 o'clock/again/probably/tomorrow morning)
    _____

5 Error spotting: Dogs in the kitchen?

Mark any mistakes you find in these sentences, and correct them by rewriting the sentences. → A, B, C

1. People on holiday in Britain like often to stay at bed and breakfast places.
   _____

2. There are all over the country a lot of B & Bs in extreme attractive surroundings.
   _____

3. The more exclusive of Britain's 20,000 B & Bs offer even "luxury" accommodation, which can be near as good as at a real nice hotel. _____
   _____

4. Some B & Bs are farmhouses, and mostly their owners have not surprisingly animals – like cats and dogs – in the house. _____
   _____

5. Visitors love generally to see these animals, and don't mind usually seeing them in the kitchen.
   _____

6. But now a newly EU rule has banned actually animals from all food preparation areas; this includes naturally kitchens. _____
   _____

Describing

7. Those who find the new rules hardliest to adapt to are farmhouse B & Bs where guests are given in the owner's kitchen their fresh cooked "English breakfast".
   _____
   _____

8. "Our two labradors sit usually in a corner of the kitchen in their baskets," says in Devon one farmhouse B & B owner. _____
   _____

9. "They behave quiet and good, and come never anywhere near where food is being prepared. Ever no guests have complained." _____
   _____

10. "The new EU rules sound to us crazily, but there's nothing we can do. We'll have to probably close," says sadly another B & B owner. _____
    _____
    _____

11. "In the kitchen is the dogs' home and, to be honest, they are to us more importantly than having guests." _____
    _____

6 What a day trip!

Add suitable adjectives and adverbs or adverbials to this description of a day trip that went wrong! (It's a true story.) You may sometimes need comparative or superlative forms. → A, B

A number of years ago, Michael and Lilian Long went over to Boulogne on a day trip one Easter Sunday. They had no idea what a/an _____ trip it would _____ turn into. _____ after they arrived at Boulogne, they went for a/an _____ walk round the town. _____ , only a/an _____ time later they were _____ lost.
"We walked such a/an _____ way!" Lilian remembered afterwards. "But we _____ couldn't find the way back! _____, our French wasn't very _____, so when we tried to ask people which way to go, they _____ didn't understand us. Whatever they answered, we had _____ no idea what they meant."
They carried on walking. But they got _____ and _____ away from Boulogne, and after walking through the night, they _____ arrived in a/an _____ village, which they did not recognize. There they _____ discovered the station and got on the _____ train, _____ expecting that it would take them _____ back to Boulogne. But they were _____ : it took them to Paris!
The Longs were _____ _____! The _____ thing they could do was to spend the rest of their money on train tickets back to Boulogne. But somehow they managed to get on the _____ train again, and by midnight on Monday they were in Luxembourg. Helped by two _____ police officers, who _____ (!) could speak _____ English, the Longs were then put on the train back to Paris. But the train divided, and the _____ couple, not knowing this, ended up in Basle, a/an _____ town in the north of Switzerland. There, they tried to find work, to finance their journey back, but _____ without success.

Describing

Feeling _____ and _____ than they had ever felt in their lives, Michael and Lilian now decided to try hitch-hiking. Their first few days on the road were _____ _____. But _____ they managed to hitch a lift to Paris. Now luck was on their side: the driver _____ dropped them off at the _____ station, and thanks to the help of three _____ tourists who were also on their way to Boulogne, the Longs _____ got on the train!

By this time, a week had passed since their 'day trip' had begun! On their arrival back in Dover after a/an _____ crossing over the English Channel, Michael Long explained that this had been their first trip abroad. He added _____ that they were _____ not intending to leave England again.

Write your comment on the story here if you wish:

In my opinion, this is a/an _____ _____ story!

7 The effect of the sound of your voice

Translate these sentences into English. Be especially aware of the differences between German and English, with regard to word order and the form of adjectives and adverbs. → A, B, C

1. Im Allgemeinen gelten gut aussehende Menschen als attraktiv. *(to be regarded as/to be considered)* _____

2. Aber ein angenehmes Aussehen ist nicht das Einzige, was darüber entscheidet, ob wir jemanden tatsächlich attraktiv finden oder nicht. *(appearance)* _____

3. Auch die Stimme und die Art und Weise, wie jemand spricht, spielen eine erstaunlich wichtige Rolle. _____

4. Oft wird angenommen, dass eine tiefe Männerstimme bei Frauen besonders gut ankommt. *(to assume; to make a good impression; male voice)* _____

5. Neulich hat eine Studie aber ein ganz anderes Ergebnis gebracht. *(to produce)* _____

6. Die meisten Frauen bevorzugen anscheinend eher höhere Männerstimmen. *(apparently)* _____

7. Am attraktivsten scheint aber eine Stimme zu sein, die selbstsicher klingt. Auch eine angenehme Sprachmelodie ist wichtig. *(self-assured; intonation)* _____

8. Sehr schnelles oder zu langsames Sprechen wirkt dagegen unattraktiv. *(to appear/seem; on the other hand)* _____

9. Machen Sie selbst einen Test, zum Beispiel wenn Sie unerwartet mit jemandem am Telefon sprechen, den Sie persönlich noch nicht kennen gelernt haben. *(test yourself)* _____

10. Klingt die Stimme für Sie angenehm oder nicht? _____

Describing

8 Making a text more interesting

*First read this anecdote. Then see how you can improve it by adding suitable adjectives, adverbs (e.g. of manner, degree, comment, frequency) or adverbials in appropriate places and rewrite it.
The extra details should make the story livelier and more interesting to read.* → A, B, C
You could start like this:

Some years ago, at an **old** English university, there was a **very small** music department with only one professor, …

> ### A useful tip?
>
> At a university, there was a music department with one professor, two assistants, and about fifteen students preparing for their degree in music. In order to get this degree, it was necessary to write a full-length concerto, symphony or choral work with orchestra.
>   One of the students, a boy called Robert, was worried about this, and he decided to go
> 5 and see his professor. He knocked on the professor's door, and the professor welcomed him and told him to sit down. He could see that Robert wasn't feeling happy.
>   "I've got a problem," Robert said. "I can do the history of music, I'm OK with the theory and I can manage the counterpoint. But I can't write a full-length work! I'm not a composer! What shall I do?"
> 10   The professor looked at him and smiled. "I've heard that story before, my boy!" he said. "And I have a solution to your problem. It's simple. All you have to do is this: Find a symphony or a concerto by a 20th century composer. Choose one that you like, but it shouldn't be a well-known work. Buy the score, and copy it out backwards. It will look convincing, you can be sure! The examiners won't notice what you've done. Get it bound –
> 15 because they like it to look professional, that's important. Then you should be all right, OK?"
>   Robert was amazed. He thanked the professor for this idea, and left. He had begun to feel better. What a tip! He was so grateful for the advice that he decided to go out and buy the score of a symphony that his professor had composed: his one and only published symphony!
> 20   Robert didn't know whether it had been performed or not, but he was sure it wasn't a well-known work. It should be ideal!
>   Robert spent the summer vacation copying the symphony out backwards. It wasn't until he had finished that he realized he had a hand-written copy of Sibelius's 4th symphony.
>
> Antony Hopkins, in: *My Lords, Ladies and Gentlemen*, 1986

8 **counterpoint** technique of combining melodies according to set rules • 13 **score** *Partitur*

9 Choosing the right non-finite verb form

There are **finite** and **non-finite** verb forms in English. The **finite** verb forms give you information as to the grammatical person (*I*, *you*, *she* etc.), the number (*singular* or *plural*) or the tense (*present*, *past*, *future* etc.).
Non-finite verb forms give you no such information.
The **infinitive**, the **gerund** and the **participle** are **non-finite** verb forms.

finite verb form	
Amy **plays** volleyball.	→ 3rd person → singular → simple present
non-finite verb forms	
Amy wants **to play** volleyball on Saturday. Amy enjoys **playing** volleyball. I often watch Amy **playing** volleyball.	→ infinitive → gerund → participle

A The infinitive

Basic rules

Expressing wishes and expectations, commands and advice

The **infinitive** is often used after verbs that express a wish or an expectation (e.g. *expect, hope, intend, plan, want, would like*, etc.). In this case the infinitive refers to something that may happen in the future.	Randy **wants to be** a musician. He **intends to form** a rock group.
Want, wish, would like and *expect* can be followed by an **object + infinitive construction**.	Randy's parents **would like their son to become** a lawyer. They **expect him to do** well at school and **go** to university.
After certain expressions (*It is important, There is no need* etc.), you can use a construction with **for + object + infinitive**. In German a *dass*-clause is very often used here.	It is important **for young people to decide** on the right career. But there is no need **for us to worry** about that yet. Es ist wichtig, **dass** sich junge Menschen für den richtigen Beruf **entscheiden**.
The **verb + object + infinitive** construction can also be used to express commands, advice or warnings. This construction corresponds to an **indirect command**. It is often used after *ask, advise, remind, tell, warn* etc.	The driving instructor **told Steve to put** his seat belt on before starting the engine. She **advised everyone to pay** special attention to cyclists.

Different from German:

German sentences like *Ich will, dass …* or *Ich möchte, dass …* can **only** be translated by the **object + infinitive** construction:

Randy will/möchte, dass seine Eltern ihn unterstützen. → Randy wants his parents to support him.
Er möchte, dass sie Vertrauen zu ihm haben. → He'd like them to have confidence in him.

> **Tip**
> You **mustn't** use a clause with *that* … after *want* or *would like*.

78

Choosing the right non-finite verb form

Basic rules

Causing and allowing – *make* **and** *let* **+ infinitive for German** *'lassen'*

Veranlassen:

make **someone do something**
You can use *make* + object + infinitive without *to* to say that someone (*the coach*) forces someone else to do something or that something (*success*) causes something to happen.

After their defeat on Saturday the coach **made the players work** extra hard the next week.
Success always **makes us feel** more confident.

Zulassen:

let **someone do something**
You can use *let* + object + infinitive without *to* to say that someone **allows** someone to do something or allows something to happen.

Mrs Bates usually **lets Sandra do** what she wants in the holidays.
But she **doesn't let her stay out** all night.

Using the infinitive after question words and after *the first, the last, the only one*

Instead of a subordinate clause with a question word followed by *should, can, must, could* or *have to*, you can use a shorter construction with a **question word + infinitive**.

Students often wonder how they can improve their English.
= Students often wonder **how to improve** their English.

Question words like *how, where, when, what, who, whether* etc. are often used after *wonder, (not) know, tell, remember, decide,* etc. The **infinitive construction** is shorter and more common than the corresponding subordinate clause.

I can't decide whether I should spend a year in the States or not.
= I can't decide **whether to spend** a year in the States or not.

The **infinitive** is also used after expressions like *the first, the last* and *the only one/ones*. This construction corresponds to a relative clause.

Johnny Weissmüller was **the first** (man) **to swim** the 100 metres in less than one minute.
= … the first (man) who swam …

The first and **the last** can be used with or without a noun. **The only** must be followed by a noun (*person/actor*) or by the prop word *one/ones*.

But he wasn't **the only person/man/actor/one to play** the role of Tarzan.
= … the only one who played …

Tip
There are two more ways of expressing German *lassen*:
1. *have* + direct object + past participle:
   I had that photo taken for my passport.
2. *leave*
   Please *leave* me alone.

(For **"verbs of perception + infinitive"** see **C The participle**)

Wow, your parents let you stay up all night!

"First they make you button your own shirt, then they make you tie your own shoes… you gotta ask yourself – where's this all heading?"

Choosing the right non-finite verb form

1 Things people want and expect

First decide who you think is speaking. Then choose from the verbs on the right to explain what the various people want or expect. Use as many different verbs as you can. → A

Speaker: our neighbours • the police • Jim's mother • Sarah's driving instructor • doctors • Lucy's parents • our English teacher • Harry's piano teacher

Verb: advise – ask – expect – remind – tell – want – warn – would like

1. "It would be nice if you could tidy your room more often." _____
2. "Never leave valuables in your car." _____
3. "It's always a good idea to read your work through before you give it in." _____
4. "You needn't help us in the garden." _____
5. "Please cancel in good time if you can't keep an appointment." _____
6. "Please don't let your visitors park in front of our garage." _____
7. "Don't forget to look in the mirror before overtaking." _____
8. "Do try to practise every day!" _____

2 How important is it?

Use these ideas to write 8–10 sentences expressing your own opinion. → A

Examples: It's important for young people to be given a good education.

important (not) necessary (not) unusual/normal right/wrong/best easy/hard understandable	for	pets animals in the wild young people/teenagers/small children girls/boys parents teachers/schools politicians developing countries

Choosing the right non-finite verb form

3 Making and letting

a) *Say it differently – with **let** or **make**, according to the situation.* → A

Example:
I'm sometimes allowed to drive my mother's car.
→ My mother sometimes **lets me drive** her car.

But I don't have to pay for the petrol.
→ But she **doesn't make me pay** for the petrol.

1. I'm never allowed to smoke in the house, because my parents are against it.

2. I don't often have to help my father in the garden.

3. I don't like it if people try to force me to do things.

4. My diary is absolutely private – nobody will ever be allowed to read it!

5. My brother takes guitar lessons. He's usually allowed to choose the pieces he wants to play.

b) **Make** + infinitive is often used to describe the **effect** something has, e.g. "Alan's jokes always make me laugh!"
Using the verbs in the box on the right, say what effect these things – or people – have on you. → A

> think …
> want to …
> feel …
> feel like … -ing …
> wonder …
> wish …
> hope …

1. The sound of the alarm clock early in the morning

2. The first snow

3. Seeing someone in a wheelchair

4. The fact that there is so much poverty in the world

5. Sad films always

6. The smell of meat grilling on a barbecue

7. The sight of the sea on a warm summer's day

8. Predictions of climate change

9. The thought that I'll soon be leaving school

10. Listening to my favourite music

Choosing the right non-finite verb form

4 Expressing ideas with different infinitive constructions

Rephrase what these people say, using infinitive constructions. A passive infinitive may sometimes be needed. → A

1. I'll probably go to university after I leave school. – I'm planning _____

2. I need your help with these heavy bags. – I'd like _____
3. Daniel is never allowed to ride his father's racing bike. – Daniel's father _____

4. Take this medicine – then you'll feel better. – This medicine will _____
5. You needn't worry about your exams. – There's no need _____
6. My tennis coach says I ought to practise more regularly. My tennis coach tells _____

7. We always have to do masses of work for German. – Our German teacher _____

8. Which shoes shall I wear for Judy's wedding? – I can't decide _____

9. I hope I'll be accepted at Exeter University. – I hope _____
10. White wine ought to be served cool. – It's important _____
11. Not many people helped with the clearing up after my party. Only John and Melissa did. – John and Melissa _____
12. Children in the UK are quite often sent to boarding school. – It's not unusual _____

Choosing the right non-finite verb form

5 Helpful people and useful things

Explain how these people and things can help. Use question words and infinitives to express your ideas. → A

Example: A TV guide is useful if you're wondering **what programme to watch/whether to watch anything on TV/when to switch your favourite programmes on.**

1. If you're driving to a place where you've never been before, a navigation system can show you _____

2. A travel agent may be able to help you if you can't quite decide _____

3. If you've just bought a new mobile, you'll probably need to read the instructions to find out _____

4. If you're lost in the middle of a strange town or city, a pedestrian may be able to tell you _____

5. If you have to give a presentation, there are useful books on _____

6. When you're on holiday, listening to the weather forecast can often help you to decide _____

7. You'll need to look at a recipe book if you don't know _____

8. At British schools, there's a careers officer to help pupils who are wondering _____

9. Reading film reviews can be a help if you're not sure _____

B The gerund

Basic rules

The gerund after certain verbs

A number of verbs can be followed by a **gerund** or an **infinitive**: *like, love, prefer, hate* as well as *begin, start* and *continue*. As there is practically no difference in meaning, it doesn't really matter which **non-finite** form you use after them.

Tracy **likes going/likes to go** shopping with her friends at weekends.
Her brother Tom **prefers doing/prefers to do** sports with his friends at the leisure centre.

However, some verbs can only be followed by a **gerund**, and it is important for you to remember them: *avoid, can't stand, enjoy, finish, imagine, involve, keep, (not) mind, miss, risk.*

Tracy **can't imagine living** in a small village.
Living in the country **involves commuting** to work every day.
Some people **don't mind travelling** long distances.

The gerund after prepositions

The **gerund** is used after **verbs, adjectives** or **nouns** that are followed by *prepositions* (*talk about, look forward to, afraid of, interested in, the idea of, difficulty in,* etc.)

Tracy's parents sometimes **talk about moving** to the country.
But they are **afraid of losing** their friends in the city.
And they don't like **the idea of living** far away from the rest of the family.

> **Tip**
> After *would like* and *would love* only the infinitive can be used:
> *Where would you like to spend your holidays?*
> *I'd love to go to Australia.*

> **Tip**
> Be careful with *look forward to* and *be/get used to*. The *to* in these constructions is not part of the infinitive but a **preposition** followed by a gerund:
> *I'm looking forward to starting work next week.*
> *I'm quite used to working in a team.*

> **Tip**
> After *way, chance* and *opportunity* you can use the *infinitive* or *of + gerund*.
> *What's the best way to deal with this?/of dealing with this?*

Choosing the right non-finite verb form

Basic rules

Gerund or infinitive? (Difference in meaning)

There are a few verbs that can be followed either by a **gerund** or an **infinitive** – but with a **difference in meaning**. Basically the **gerund** refers to something that has come to an end while the **infinitive** refers to something that is still to be done.

Gerund	**Infinitive**
After *forget* and *remember* the **gerund** describes an event or activity that has already taken place:	After *forget* and *remember* the **infinitive** expresses an intention to do something new:
I'll never **forget seeing** Alex on stage the first time. Do you **remember meeting** him after the performance?	I mustn't **forget to buy** his biography. Please **remember to book** tickets in time.
After *stop* the **gerund** refers to something that has come to an end:	After *stop* the **infinitive** refers to a new activity:
I've now **stopped sending** him a card on Valentine's Day.	When I saw him in town, he actually **stopped to talk** to me.
After *mean* the **gerund** describes a logical consequence:	After *mean* the **infinitive** expresses an intention to do something:
If we really want to go to his next show in Cardiff, it'll **mean staying** the night somewhere. (…, bedeutet das, dass …)	I **mean to ask** him for his autograph next time I see him. (… ich habe vor/beabsichtige …)

6 All about cycling

Complete the text with gerunds or infinitives, deciding where a preposition is needed. → A, B

In 2008, Washington DC became the first U.S. city _____ (start) an automated bicycle-sharing programme. The programme, which is called SmartBike DC, was originally planned _____ (reduce) traffic congestion and pollution but it naturally also helps _____ (solve) parking problems. It is ideal for people who are tired _____ (wait) for buses or fed up _____ (sit) in crowded subway trains. If you want _____ (use) one of the bikes, you need _____ (have) a membership card. For $40 a year, you can then enjoy _____ (ride) a 3-speed bicycle anywhere in the city for up to three hours at one time. Although it is not possible _____ (provide) helmets as part of the programme, members are strongly recommended _____ (use) them.

Choosing the right non-finite verb form

At the same time, the question of whether _____ (make) helmets compulsory for cyclists was being discussed a lot in Britain. Although _____ (wear) a helmet can often prevent cyclists _____ (injure) their heads in an accident, there is also evidence that in Australia and New Zealand, where the law makes it compulsory for all cyclists _____ (wear) helmets, the risk _____ (have) an accident has actually increased! One reason for this seems _____ (be) that motorists generally avoid _____ (drive) too close to cyclists <u>without</u> helmets! Another aspect is that _____ (wear) a helmet makes cyclists _____ (feel) safer, which actually makes them more likely _____ (ride) faster and _____ (take) more risks.

It is also a fact that in countries with 'compulsory helmet' laws, a lot of people have stopped _____ (cycle) altogether (because they don't like the thought _____ (wear) a helmet!). Women, especially, tend _____ (dislike) _____ (wear) helmets. More than half of British women aged 18 to 34 actually refuse _____ (cycle) to work because they are worried _____ (look) less attractive when they arrive! A study claims that 27% are concerned about their hairstyles _____ (be spoilt) by the helmets, while 58% are afraid _____ (get) hot and sweaty.

Interestingly, in the Netherlands, where people are traditionally very fond _____ (cycle), only 1% of cyclists wear a helmet, yet the risk _____ (be hurt) in a cycling accident there is lower than anywhere else in the world.

compulsory [kəmˈpʌlsəri]: necessary (because the law says so)

7 Remembering and forgetting ...

a) *Decide which fits the situation: gerund or infinitive?* → B

1. Don't forget _____ (take) the cake out of the oven for me!
2. You can tell she's in love with Andrew – she can't stop _____ (talk) about him!
3. I've been meaning _____ (discuss) this problem with you for ages, but there's never been a suitable opportunity.
4. Was Carlos really at Sonia's party? I don't remember _____ (see) him.
5. I'm sorry you're so upset about what I said. I didn't mean _____ (hurt) your feelings!

b) *Now rewrite these sentences, using the verbs in brackets, followed by gerunds or infinitives according to the situation.* → B

1. I don't like it when you interrupt me all the time! (stop) – Please _____
   _____

2. If you really want to work as a model, you'll have to travel up to London a lot. (mean)
   Working as a model _____

3. Oh dear, I'm afraid I didn't switch the heating off. (forget) – I _____

4. I'd like you to close all the windows before you leave the house, OK? (remember) – Please
   _____

5. Why don't we park here for a moment, so we can enjoy the view? (stop) – Let's _____
   _____

6. It was an incredible moment when I met Prince William at that party in London! (forget)
   – I'll never _____

Choosing the right non-finite verb form

C The participle and the infinitive after verbs of perception

> **Basic rules**
>
> Verbs such as *feel, hear, find, notice, observe, see* and *watch* are verbs of perception. After these verbs + direct object it is possible to use the present participle, and also the infinitive without *to*:
>
> | **verb of perception + direct object + present participle** | **verb of perception + direct object + infinitive without *to*** |
> |---|---|
> | We **were watching** our neighbour **cutting** his hedge. | Then we suddenly **saw** him **fall** off his ladder. |
>
> In German these constructions correspond to an infinitive construction or to a subordinate clause with 'wie': … sahen wir ihn plötzlich … fallen./… sahen wir, wie er plötzlich … fiel.
>
> These two constructions are used differently.
> - The **present participle** describes an **activity in progress**. Only part of the action is seen or heard.
> - The **infinitive** describes a **completed action**. It is seen from its beginning to its end. This is especially the case when the activity is short or when a series of actions are described.
>
> | **present participle:** activity in progress  | **infinitive:** completed activity |
> |---|---|
> | We **saw** Mr Green **climbing** a tall ladder. Then we **watched** him carefully **trimming** the top of his hedge. | Suddenly we **noticed** his ladder **slip**. We saw him **drop** his cutter and **crash** to the ground; then we **heard** him **shout** out in pain. |
> | Here, the **present participle** corresponds to the **progressive form**: *Mr Green was trimming his hedge.* | Here, the **infinitive** corresponds to the **simple form**: *His ladder slipped.* |

8 What they noticed

Complete the sentences, choosing from the verbs in the boxes, and deciding whether to use participles or infinitives. → C

put
leave
whisper
work
look
walk
stand
wait
giggle

1. *Julie:* When I went into the shop, I noticed a lot of people _____ at the latest DVDs. I saw two shop assistants _____ busily behind the counter and several customers _____ to be served. Not far from where I was, I could see two girls _____ very close together. I could hear them _____ and _____ , but I couldn't make out what they were saying. Then, quite unexpectedly, I noticed one of them _____ the DVD she was holding into a shoulder-bag, and before I could react, I saw the two of them _____ quickly past the counter and _____ the shop.

laugh
sit (2x)
smile
touch
come
talk

2. *Will:* I was at the cinema the other day. After I'd found my place, I watched quite a few people _____ in and _____ down in the rows in front of me, but I didn't recognize anyone. When the film had started, I heard a man and a woman in the row behind me _____ to each other in low voices. It was a comedy we were watching, and when I heard the woman suddenly _____ , I thought her voice sounded somehow familiar, but I didn't look round. When the lights came on after the film, I felt someone _____ my shoulder and, turning round, I saw two well-known faces _____ at me. It was Sally and Mike, two old schoolfriends I hadn't seen for ages. They had noticed me _____ in front of them and had recognized me.

Choosing the right non-finite verb form

9 Translation: What's that in English?

How can you put these everyday German sentences into good English? → A, C
Remember that constructions with non-finite verbs forms are often used where you would find a 'dass' clause or other subordinate clause in German.

1. Meine Eltern wollen nicht, dass ich abends spät nach Hause komme.
   _____

2. Möchtest du, dass ich dir helfe? _____

3. Ich weiß nicht, was ich machen soll. Ich kann mich einfach nicht entscheiden, ob ich das Angebot annehmen soll oder nicht. _____

4. Niemand kann erwarten, dass wir Tag und Nacht an diesem Projekt arbeiten!
   _____

5. Belinda wartet immer noch darauf, dass Tim sie anruft. _____

6. Es ist wichtig, dass Haustiere versorgt werden, wenn man verreist.
   _____

7. Du bist immer der erste, der meckert! *(complain, grumble)* _____

8. Meine Mutter lässt es nicht zu, dass ich sonntags den ganzen Tag im Bett bleibe.
   _____

9. Habt ihr gestern gesehen, wie die neuen Nachbarn eingezogen sind?
   _____

10. Mein Vater möchte, dass ich Arzt oder Zahnarzt werde, aber ich finde es nicht richtig, dass Eltern über die Zukunft ihrer Kinder bestimmen. _____

10 A cartoon: What he wants for Christmas

a) *Describe the cartoon. Why is it funny?* → C
b) *What else do you often see/notice/hear happening during the weeks before Christmas?* → C
c) *Make up three more things the boy could wish for, using non-finite constructions.* → A

"Oh, I almost forgot, and the polar ice caps. I want them to stop melting."

Useful phrases

Describing cartoons
It shows … • In the middle/centre of the picture there is … • at the top/bottom • on the left/right • to the left/right of … • in the top left-hand/bottom right-hand corner • in the background/foreground • There is a contrast between … • … is clearly visible • The focus is on… • The colours are bright/dark. • This creates an … atmosphere. … • The artist aims to …

Choosing the right non-finite verb form

11 Work experience in the UK

J17, a British magazine for teenagers, advertised these examples of work experience placements in the UK – as part of a competition. Anyone interested could apply for the placement they hoped to win.

business

Birmingham
Top Shop
We don't need to tell you how great *Top Shop* is! A placement here would involve working in all parts of the store from the stock room to the shop floor. You'll learn all about the latest fashions, stock control and displaying clothes. You'll also get the chance to practise your best customer service skills.

Apply if: You are polite, have good customer service skills and are interested in fashion.

Cardiff
The Body Shop
This is a great opportunity for anyone wanting to work in retail or the beauty and cosmetics industry. The Body Shop is famous for its naturally-based products and is committed to campaigning against human rights abuses, promoting animal protection and challenging stereotypes of beauty within the cosmetics industry.

Apply if: You want to work in retail management and are interested in the beauty industry.

community work

Newcastle
Going for Green
Going For Green is a national charity that campaigns to improve the environment. It encourages people to get together and carry out things like sponsored events, clean-up operations and generally raise awareness. This is a great job for anyone who doesn't mind donning their wellies and really getting stuck in.

Apply if: You are interested in green issues and aren't afraid to get your hands dirty.

Manchester
Signets to Swans
This day nursery caters for 20 children aged three months to two years old. It's a brilliant opportunity for anyone interested in working with children – whether as a nanny or as a nursery school teacher. You will be shadowing a member of staff, observing the many activities that the children get involved in from painting to using sand, water and playdough.

Apply if: You love working with children and want to learn more about nursery school teaching.

science

Newcastle
Boots the Chemist
What girl wouldn't want to spend time with a company whose aim is to make you look good and feel good? There are a number of experts working within the Boots stores, from pharmacists and chiropodists to health and beauty advisers. During your placement you'll get an all-round experience of working in a health and beauty environment.

Apply if: You are interested in science and have good communication skills.

Birmingham
West Midlands Health Research Unit
This is the perfect starting point for anyone who wants to get into the medical profession. The unit produces a quarterly magazine and also trains students. This placement involves researching projects, and looking after the in-house library and Internet facility, which is open to the public.

Apply if: You enjoy working on your own projects and are interested in a career in health or medicine.

creative

Edinburgh
The Scotsman
If you fancy trying out the frenzied world of regional journalism, then there's no better place to start than *The Scotsman*. It's one of the biggest papers in Scotland and a placement here will give you a good idea of working life in the media. You'll get to spend time in the busy editorial department following stories, and could even shadow a reporter chasing that big scoop.

Apply if: You are motivated, enthusiastic and good at coming up with ideas.

Cardiff
Wood & Wood Design
This is a graphic design consultancy that produces leaflets, adverts and promotional material for other companies. As it's a small company, this is a great opportunity for someone who is interested in design to really get stuck in. You will be set a project for the week, and taught how to use the software.

Apply if: You like working on your own initiative and have a keen interest in art and design.

Choosing the right non-finite verb form 9

a) *First read the descriptions of the placements on offer. Then mark (or underline) examples of constructions involving* infinitives *or* gerunds. *Next, write some of the examples you have found in the appropriate place in the grid:* → A, B

Infinitive after verbs expressing wishes, expectations, needs, etc.	
Verb + object + infinitive with 'to'	
Infinitive after nouns	
'for' + object + infinitive	
'make' or 'let' + infinitive without 'to'	
Gerund as object after verbs	
Gerund after verbs, adjectives or nouns + preposition	
Infinitive after a question word	

b) *Choose the 'career type' you personally find most interesting (business, community work, science, creative work), and compare the two placements on offer for this 'type'. Then explain which you would prefer to do, pointing out the advantages and disadvantages of the two, and why you think one of them would be more suitable for you personally. Use some of these verbs / expressions:*
→ A, B

would like to … – have always wanted to … – enjoy … – would look forward to … – good at … – not so good at … – hopeless at … – interested in … – the thought of … makes me (feel) … – a chance/ an opportunity for me to …

Using the articles

10 Using the articles

A The definite article

In general, the use of the definite and the indefinite article in English is similar to the way the articles are used in German.

Before nouns that are used in a general sense there is **no definite article**.
*Without **water**, there would be no life on earth.*

The **definite article** is used when you describe a particular case.
*In recent years **the water** in the Thames has become much cleaner.*

With some nouns you use the **definite article** differently in English:

Basic rules

Nouns used in a general sense: without *the*	Nouns describing a particular case: with *the*
Abstract ideas	
You don't use an article before abstract nouns, e.g. *life*, *time*, when you refer to things in general. This is also the case when an adjective is used in front of the noun (*modern history*).	You need to use an article when these nouns are defined more closely, e.g. by an *of* phrase (*of man, of the Labour Party*) or a relative clause (*we spent together*).
*Stop quarrelling, **life** is too short for that.* (… **das Leben** …)	*Thomas Hobbes said that in the state of nature "**the life** of man is solitary, poor, nasty, brutish, and short."*
***Time** flies when you're having fun.* (**Die Zeit** …) *I'm more interested in **modern history** than in the ancient Greeks and Romans.* (… für **die neuere Geschichte** …)	*Can you still remember **the time** we spent together at summer camp?* *I'd like to write a thesis on **the history** of the Labour Party.*
Means of transport	
There is no article when you refer to the type of transport in general.	You use the definite article when you refer to a particular vehicle.
*I quite enjoy travelling by **bus**.* (… mit **dem Bus** …) *My father has to go to work by **train**.* (… mit **dem Zug** …)	*There were very few people on **the bus** this morning.* ***The train** to Dover will be 10 minutes late.*
Institutions	
You don't use an article when you refer to the function of an institution, e.g *school = lessons*.	You use the article when you refer to a particular building.
*Rob doesn't like **school** much.* … **die Schule** … *Do you often go to **church**?* … in **die Kirche**?	***The school** he goes to hasn't got a very good reputation.* ***The church** in the village was built in the 16th century.*
Meals	
When you refer to meals in general, not thinking of the food eaten at a particular meal, you don't use an article.	When you refer to a particular meal, you use the definite article.
***Breakfast** is my favourite meal.* **Das Frühstück** … *What did you have for **lunch**?* *We had **dinner** at the Red Lion on Mum's birthday.*	*I really enjoyed **the breakfast** at that Swiss hotel.* ***The lunch** you cooked yesterday was delicious!* *Who paid for **the dinner** at the Red Lion?*

Using the articles 10

There are special rules for the use of the definite article with names:

Basic rules	
Names (singular)	**Names (plural)**
There is no article before singular names, even if an adjective (*poor*) comes before the name.	Surnames in the plural are used with the definite article.
Poor Judy had to go to hospital. **Die arme Judy** …	*The Millers* have invited *the Carters* to their party. **(Die) Millers** … **(die) Carters** …

B The indefinite article

There are only a few cases where the **indefinite article** in English is used differently from the way it is used in German:

Basic rules	
Jobs	
*Janice would love to be **an actress**.* *But her parents would prefer it if she became **a doctor** or **a lawyer**.*	… möchte sehr gerne **Schauspielerin** werden. … würden es vorziehen, wenn sie **Ärztin** oder **Rechtsanwältin** werden würde.
Nationality and religion/after 'as'	
*Christopher Columbus was **an Italian**, although some historians consider him to have been **a Spaniard**.* *Columbus was certainly **a Catholic**.* *Even **as a small boy** he was interested in the sea and navigation.*	… war **Italiener**. … dass er **Spanier** war. … war … **Katholik**. … als kleiner Junge …
Certain phrases	
*I don't feel too good today. I've got **a headache** and **a temperature**.* *She's always in **a hurry**.*	… **Kopfschmerzen** und **Fieber**. … in Eile.
Equivalent to 'per'	
*This South African wine costs £12 **a bottle**.* *There's a speed limit of 70 miles **an hour** on the motorway.* *I usually see the dentist twice **a year**.*	… pro Flasche / die Flasche. … 70 Meilen pro Stunde … … pro Jahr / im Jahr.

> **Tip**
> When you refer to a person's nationality, you can, of course, use an adjective instead of a noun:
> *Christopher Columbus was **Italian** (or **Spanish**?) and his wife was **Portuguese**.*

Columbus discovers that when exploring, it's not such a great idea to bring the family along.

1 A cartoon: Columbus at sea

What else might the members of Columbus's family say?
Try to include sentences with/without the definite or indefinite article. → A, B

Example: *Why didn't we go by plane, Dad?*

10 Using the articles

C The position of the articles

Just like in German, the definite and indefinite articles usually come before an adjective + noun (*the old story, an old story*). But there are a few exceptions to this rule:

Basic rules

Definite article after *all, both, double, half, twice*

All the guests enjoyed the party.	**Alle** Gäste …
Both the hosts made everyone very welcome.	**Beide** Gastgeber …
As there were so many extra people, **double the** amount of food and drink had to be ordered.	… **die doppelte** Menge …
In the end there was so much to eat that **half the** food was left.	… **das halbe** Essen …
It could have served **twice the** number of guests.	… **die doppelte** Anzahl …

Basic rules

Indefinite article after *half, quite, such, what*

Let's rest for **half an** hour.	… **eine halbe** Stunde.
It's been **quite a** strenuous hike.	… **eine ziemlich** anstrengende Wanderung.
I hadn't expected it to be **such a** long way.	… **ein solch/so** langer Weg …
But **what a** breathtaking view we had from the top!	… **was für eine** atemberaubende Aussicht …

2 With or without *the*?

*Complete the sentences, deciding whether or not you need to use the **definite article**.* → A

1. Are you planning to go to _____ university when you leave _____ school? – Definitely. I want to study _____ philosophy, if possible at _____ Exeter University, so I won't be too far away from home. And you? – I'm hoping to go to _____ London School of Economics.

2. What shall we have for _____ lunch today? – Let's try out one of the recipes from my new book. '_____ Real Indian Cooking'. – OK, I love _____ Asian food! But let's choose something that's easy to make. – Look, what about this? 'Bombay Chicken with _____ rice and _____ mango chutney'. – Mm! Sounds almost as good as _____ food we had at the 'Taj Mahal' last week!

3. What's that book you're reading? – It's about _____ life in Britain at _____ time of _____ Tudors. At _____ moment I'm reading a chapter on _____ life of Elizabeth _____ First, and _____ influence she had on _____ English history.

4. Have you heard about _____ poor Tom's accident? – No, what happened? – Well, you know he always goes everywhere by _____ bike. Anyway, yesterday, after _____ school, he was involved in an accident with _____ school bus. It happened just near _____ church, I don't know how! Now he's in _____ hospital with a broken leg. – Who told you? – Our neighbours, _____ McPhersons. Mrs McPherson works at _____ hospital.

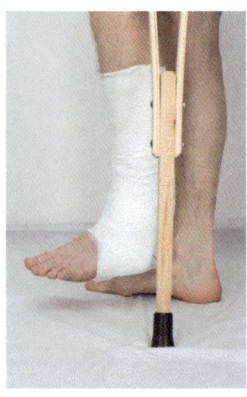

Using the articles 10

3 Talking about people

a) *Use the right **nouns** to explain what jobs these people have or are interested in, what beliefs they have, or where they are from.* → B

Example: My brother has just finished medical school. Now he's **a doctor.**

1. J.K. Rowling writes books. She's _____.
2. My sister has always been interested in the latest hairstyles. Now she's training to be _____.
3. The Dalai Lama believes in the teachings of Buddha. He _____.
4. Susan goes to Mass every Sunday. She _____.
5. Joe lives in Toronto. He _____.
6. His wife originally comes from Cape Town. She _____.
7. Kate's little brother loves playing with model planes. When he's big, he says he wants to be _____.
8. My father doesn't believe in any religion of any kind. He calls himself _____.

b) *Now write descriptions to fit 6 of these nouns. (Refer to a dictionary if you need to.)*

Example: Someone who always expects the worst is a pessimist.

> individualist – idealist – agnostic – perfectionist – pessimist – democrat – cynic – communist – royalist – capitalist – pacifist – feminist – optimist – patriot – realist

4 Dialogues

*Use phrases with **half, such, quite, what, all** or **twice**, together with **a/an** or **the**, to help complete these short dialogues.* → C
Choose from the words on the right.

piece: half	price: twice
shock: quite	night: half
hour: half ✓	hurry: such
surprise: what	food: all

1. How long did it take you to walk here?
   Not long. It only took me half an hour.

2. How did you feel when you were told you'd lost your job?
   _____

3. Is the cake OK? Do have some more!
   _____

4. Hi there! May I come in? We haven't seen each other for ages, have we?
   _____

5. Oh dear, isn't there anything left for us to eat?
   _____

6. I got a really cheap ticket for the show tonight. It only cost £15! What about you?
   _____

7. I hope you didn't have to stay up too long to finish that essay of yours.
   _____

8. You forgot your mobile when you left the house this morning!
   _____

10 Using the articles

5 Can we feed the world?

Complete the text – where necessary – with the definite and indefinite article. → A, B, C

Back in _____ 18th century Thomas Malthus, _____ English parson, was _____ first to give _____ scientific weight to _____ theory that
5 _____ unchecked population growth, combined with _____ dwindling supplies of _____ food, would lead to _____ 'gigantic famine' and eventually to _____ extinction of _____ mankind.

10 Malthus was seen as _____ pessimist, and has often been described as _____ doom-monger. But his theory has often been discussed at times of food shortages, for _____ example at _____ time of _____ Irish potato famine. More recently, in 2008, when _____ price of _____ food led to riots in Haiti and Cairo, _____ UN warned that _____ grain production must rise at least 50% by _____ year 2030 if
15 _____ global hunger is to be averted.

It is generally expected that _____ population of _____ planet will grow from over six and _____ half billion today to over nine billion by 2050. How can we possibly hope to feed such _____ incredible number of _____ people? _____ problem is made worse by _____ fact that vast areas of _____ land have been given over to
20 _____ production of biofuels. 25% of _____ US maize crop may be made into ethanol by 2020, which is seen by some as _____ way of making _____ USA less dependent on _____ oil. Others protest against _____ idea of 'wasting' _____ good land in this way.

In quite _____ number of _____ world's wealthiest countries, population levels
25 have fallen, but at _____ same time _____ demand for _____ food has risen, because people are – on _____ average – eating _____ lot more than their bodies need. (They are also buying more than they need: in _____ United Kingdom, we throw away 6.7 million tonnes of food _____ year, worth about eight billion pounds. What _____ waste!) Whereas 850 million people exist in _____ permanent state of
30 _____ malnourishment, _____ even larger number of _____ people worldwide are now obese!

In _____ coming years and decades, _____ key shortage is likely to be _____ water. So _____ problem of too little _____ water for _____ farming may have to be solved by boosting _____ production of genetically modified (GM) crops that can grow
35 even on _____ dry soil. Such _____ solution may not sound ideal (and _____ most people in _____ Europe are against it). But if _____ alternative is _____ hunger, we aren't going to have much choice.

2 **parson** [ˈpɑːsən]: a Christian priest or minister • 6 **to dwindle** [ˈdwɪndl]: to become less and less or smaller and smaller • 10 **doom-monger** [ˈduːmˌmʌŋɡə]: someone who prophesies disaster • 15 **to avert** [əˈvɜːt]: to prevent (sth unpleasant) from happening • 30 **malnourishment** [mælˈnʌrɪʃmənt]: not having enough good food to eat • 31 **obese** [əʊˈbiːs]: dangerously overweight

Using the articles 10

6 What's that in English? → A, B, C

1. Mein Bruder ist Schauspieler, aber im Moment arbeitet er als Kellner.

2. Das Leben kann manchmal schwer sein, aber man darf die Hoffnung nie aufgeben.

3. Die meisten meiner Freunde fahren mit dem Bus zur Schule.

4. Ich warte seit über einer halben Stunde hier vor der Schule auf dich! Was hast du die ganze Zeit gemacht?

5. Heute abend kommt ein Film im Fernsehen über die Evolution und das Leben von Charles Darwin. Es könnte eine ganz spannende Sendung sein.

6. Warum spielt die Technik eine so wichtige Rolle in der heutigen Gesellschaft?

7 Mediation: A Heavy Metal Catholic

Write a letter to an English-speaking friend telling him/her in simple English about the content of this article and commenting on Julian's views. First mark the passages you find important. → A, B, C

MUSIK SCHLÄGT KIRCHE – Wie ein Messdiener zum Metal-Fan wurde

Julian Rohrer war Ministrant in der Kirche, doch abends drosch der 23-Jährige am liebsten in schwarzer Kluft auf seine Gitarre ein. Er wollte Diener Gottes sein und gleichzeitig die Welt mit seiner Heavy-Metal-Musik aufrütteln. Das ging nicht lange gut.

Der Ort, an dem Julians Band „Waldwind" in der heutigen kühlen Herbstnacht probt, ist düster. Stahlzäune umgeben die leicht heruntergekommene Baracke aus Metallcontainern. Im Proberaum sind die hellen Leuchtstoffröhren mit schwarzen Tüchern bedeckt. Julian, lange schwarze Haare, ein kurzes Ziegenbärtchen und in schwarzer Lederjacke, nimmt das Plektron fest zwischen Daumen und Zeigefinger. […] Im Jahr 2000 gründete er mit einem Schulfreund seine erste Band. Hier konnte er sich mit experimentellem Rock und Heavy Metal selbst verwirklichen. Bald kam die zweite Band und mit ihr die ersten größeren Live-Auftritte: „Ich bemerkte, was Metal bedeuten und bewegen kann: Die Texte sind Rebellion, die Musik ist Unterhaltung. Damit kann ich Menschen berühren", sagt Julian Seine Begeisterung wuchs, er begann, für Musikmagazine und das Online-Portal „Powermetal" zu schreiben.

„Waldwind" ist Julians neuestes Bandprojekt. Die Musik im Proberaum klingt mal harmonisch, dann wieder erschüttern verzerrte Gitarren und kreischender Gesang den Proberaum-Container. In den Texten geht es um die Natur und ihre Gewalten – angelehnt an Textstellen aus der Bibel, die Gott und sein Wirken beschreiben. Natur und Gott gehören für Julian untrennbar zusammen. Dennoch möchte er keinen christlichen Metal machen.

[…]Dass viele Katholiken den Heavy Metal verteufeln, verstehe er nicht, sagt Julian: „Kirche und Metal, das ist beides Rebellion." Auch das Christentum habe sich immer wieder aufgelehnt gegen Unterdrückung. Was aber, wenn Metal-Fans und Kirche aufeinanderprallen, wie etwa in den neunziger Jahren in Norwegen? Black-Metal-Anhänger hatten dort 31 Kirchen angezündet. „Auf beiden Seiten gibt es fundamentalistische Spinner. In der Metal-Szene haben sie Kirchen abgebrannt, in der Kirche will man Kondome und Homosexualität verbieten", sagt Julian. Beides dürfe, findet Julian, in einer aufgeklärten Welt nicht mehr vorkommen.

Dieser Konflikt wurde zur Zerreißprobe für Julian: Die altmodischen Ansichten der Kirchen wollte er als frei denkender Metal-Fan nicht weiter unterstützen. Vor einem Jahr schmiss er die Kutte und legte sein Amt des Oberministranten in der Münchner Frauenkirche nieder: „Heute lebe ich christlich spirituell und nicht den strengen Katholizismus", sagt Julian. […]

Die christlichen Werte will er trotzdem weiter in die Welt hinaustragen. Als Diözesanleiter kümmert sich Julian ehrenamtlich um christliche Jugendfortbildungen. In Rollenspielen erarbeitet er mit Jugendgruppen, was Solidarität und christliche Werte wie Nächstenliebe bedeuten. Das ist eine Umgebung, die tolerant genug für Julians Hobby ist. Von konservativen katholischen Jugendbewegungen hält er nichts mehr: Die Gruppe „Jugend 2000" predige noch immer keinen Sex vor der Ehe. „Das kann doch nicht mehr funktionieren", sagt Julian.

Felix Scheidl, *Der Spiegel*, 16. Februar 2009

1 **Messdiener/Ministrant** altar boy • 50 **Oberministrant** head altar boy • 54 **Diözesanleiter** regional youth leader • 57 **Nächstenliebe** compassion, kindness

Using stylistic devices

Using stylistic devices

There are a number of stylistic devices which you can use to add drama to a text or to emphasize what you are saying.

A Inversion

The normal word order in an English sentence is **Subject – Verb – Object**.
In some cases, however, this word order can be changed.

Basic rules	
If a sentence begins with **hardly** (… when), **not only** (… but … also), **only after/when, never, scarcely, rarely, little, no sooner** (… than) the normal word order is changed. In this case the subject (*the ship*) comes after the auxiliary (*had*) – just as in questions. If there is no auxiliary in the sentence a form of *do* is used (*Not only **did** most of the passengers …*). This construction is called **inversion**. It is sometimes used to make a written text sound more dramatic.	**Hardly** had the ship reached the open sea **when** the weather took a turn for the worse. **Not only** did most of the passengers **begin** to feel seasick, **but** some of the crew were **also** badly affected. **Only after** we had been at sea for a week, did conditions start to improve. **Never** in my life have I had such a terrible experience. **Little** did we know what lay ahead of us when we booked that cruise.

B Emphasis

If you want to stress statements or sentence parts you can do this in a number of different ways.

Basic rules	
The *It is/It was* construction can be used to emphasize sentence parts.	
You can use *it is/it was* to emphasize any part of the sentence (except the verb).	**Original statement:** Subject Verb Object Adverbial *William the Conqueror*  *invaded* *England* *in 1066.*
The rest of the sentence follows in the form of a relative clause (*who invaded England*) or a *that* clause (*that William invaded England*).	**It was** William the Conqueror who invaded England (and not Napoleon). **It was** England that William the Conqueror invaded (and not Denmark). **It was** in 1066 that William invaded England (and not in 1077).
The singular form *it is/it was* is used even if the noun that follows is in the plural (*horsemen, events*).	**It was** the Norman horsemen that decided the Battle of Hastings. **It is** sometimes the events of only a few days that change the course of history.
This construction is normally used to emphasize a new point or to correct a mistake or misunderstanding.	Excuse me, is this the right bus for Hastings? – No, this one only goes as far as Bexhill. **It's** the number 37 that goes to Hastings.

11 Using stylistic devices

Basic rules

You can also use clauses with **what** to stress sentence parts.

What + be can be used to clarify or emphasize things.
If the direct object is emphasized, it follows **be** (… *is the lovely garden*.).
If the verb is stressed, it is replaced by a form of **do** in the first part of the sentence (… *what I usually do* …) and in the second part by an infinitive with or without *to* (… *is (to) meet* …)

I'm sorry we had to leave our old house.
***What** I miss most **is** the lovely garden.*

Grandma felt very lonely after Grandpa died.
*So **what** she **did was to get** herself a dog.*

***What** I usually **do** on a Saturday evening **is** meet my friends.*

Usually **do**, **does** and **did** are used in questions or in negative statements. But **do** can also be used to give extra emphasis to positive statements and to imperatives.

Stressing a contrast

You can use **do** to contradict a negative statement.

*Darren never helps in the garden. – Well, he **does** help sometimes. He mowed the lawn last month. Don't you remember?*
*Why didn't you call last night? – I **did** call. But nobody answered the phone.*

Stressing a request

You can use **do** before an **imperative** to make a request sound extra polite – or to express impatience.

*Hello, Mr Philips! **Do** sit down.*
***Do** help yourselves to drinks, everyone.*
*Oh, **do** switch that music off, Sam. It's driving me mad!*

Expressing a spontaneous feeling

Emphatic **do** can also express a sudden emotional reaction.
In German, adverbs like **doch, wirklich, so (sehr), ganz** or **tatsächlich** correspond to these constructions.

*I **do** hope you do well in your exams, Katie.*
*You **did** play well in concert, Tim.*
*Thanks, but I **did** feel nervous!*

C The *there* construction

Basic rules

Sentences with *be* are often introduced by **there**.

In this construction **there** is the formal subject of the sentence. It is followed by *be*, and then by the logical subject (*a new supermarket*).

*__There's__ a new supermarket in Norton Street. You know, **there** used to **be** an old factory at that corner.*

The **there** construction is also often used with present or past **participles**.
Sentences of this kind usually correspond to normal positive statements in German:
Draußen vor dem Fenster sitzt ein Eichhörnchen.

*Look, **there's** a squirrel **sitting** outside the window.*
*Oh no! **There's** a car **parked** in our driveway again.*
***There were** lots of people **queueing** for tickets before the show last night.*

11 Using stylistic devices

1 An unlucky couple

a) *Read this newspaper article, marking the examples of inversion as you go along. Notice how this stylistic device is used to add drama to the theme. (It's a true story.)* → A

Stuart, 23, and his girlfriend, Shirley, had just got engaged and were looking forward to getting married. Little did they realize what stumbling blocks and frustrations lay ahead. They were both in agreement about the church they wanted to be married in. It was a little church in Blackpool that had special memories for them. But hardly had they made their
5 choice when they received the unfortunate news that the old building was in danger of collapse and due to be demolished only a few weeks later.

Undeterred, the couple decided on a different church, and soon found a photographer to take the wedding photos. Stuart saw no need to be suspicious when the photographer insisted on being paid in advance. But no sooner had the payment been made than the
10 photographer mysteriously disappeared.

Not wanting this annoyance to spoil their happiness, the couple then booked an expensive honeymoon in the Caribbean, but shortly afterwards the tour operator went bankrupt. Not only had their honeymoon plans come to nothing, but the money they had paid in advance – several thousand pounds – was gone, too.
15 Five days before the wedding Shirley went to collect her wedding dress. Only when she tried it on at home did she realize that it was too short! Understandably, she burst into tears. Then, on the morning of the great day, there came a worried telephone call from the vicar, asking what had happened and where they were. It turned out that he had noted down the wrong time – and was expecting the ceremony to begin at 11 a.m. instead of 1 p.m.
20 Only after the church service was over did the young couple begin to relax. Later, at the reception, when their wedding cake fell on the floor, they could only laugh. "In spite of everything it was a great day!" the bride insists, looking back. "But never in my life had I dreamt that so many things could go wrong!"

2 **stumbling block** ['stʌmblɪŋ blɒk] a difficulty that stops you from achieving sth • 7 **undeterred** [ˌʌndɪ'tɜːd] not allowing sth to stop you doing what you planned • 17 **vicar** ['vɪkə] *Pfarrer (in der anglikanischen Kirche)* • 21 **(wedding) reception** [rɪ'sepʃn] a large formal party to celebrate an event (e.g. wedding)

b) *Now write your own text.* → A

Shirley/Stuart writes an informal e-mail to a friend in the USA, thanking them for a wedding present they sent – and telling them in a few sentences about the problems and difficulties the two of them experienced. (Do not use inversion, but explain what happened using normal word order.)

Using stylistic devices 11

2 Giving extra emphasis to what you say

How can you add extra emphasis to what these people say? (The words in brackets will help you.) → B

1. – I need a good strong cup of coffee now! (what)
   _____
2. – Poor you! Tell me what happened to upset you. (do)
   _____
3. – I think Amy's behaved badly. (do)
   _____
4. She's been going out with Tom, of all people! (it)
   _____
5. I don't understand how she could lie to me like that! For weeks on end! (what)
   _____
6. – You need a good friend at times like this, Philip. (what)
   _____
7. – I hoped Amy and I would stay together. (do)
   _____
8. – Never mind. Amy made a mess of the relationship, not you. (it)
   _____

3 Translating the *there* construction

The there *construction is extremely common. In German, the equivalent is sometimes 'es gibt', but very often other equivalents are used. Translate these sentences, together with a partner if possible, so you can discuss what seems to sound best.* → C

1. There's no end to the things we can do to help the environment.
   _____
2. Stop, there's a main road ahead. OK, you can go – there's nothing coming on the left.
   _____
   _____
3. I took Boxer to the vet's, but she says there's nothing the matter with him.
   _____
4. There's plenty of time for us to get to the airport from Waterloo.
   _____
5. We've got to do all the washing up by hand. There's something wrong with the dishwasher.
   _____
6. Suddenly there was a knock at the door, but when I opened it there was nobody there.
   _____
7. There was once a King who had three sons.
   _____
8. There's no point in worrying about things we can't change.
   _____
9. There are many more women working in politics *(tätig sein)* today than there used to be.
   _____
10. There must be some way of solving the problem.
    _____

A Appendix

Grammatical terms

adjective 8	Robert is a **good** friend.	Adjektiv
adjectives after verbs	He **looks good** in his new coat.	Adjektiv nach Verben
adjectives as nouns?	**The rich are lucky**.	Adjektiv als Nomen
adverb / adverbial 8		Adverb/adverbiale Bestimmung
~ of degree	It's **very** late.	Gradadverb
~ of comment	**Of course** I like her.	kommentierendes Adverb
~ of frequency	I **always** get up early.	~ der Häufigkeit
~ of manner	**quickly, easily, in a friendly way**, etc.	~ der Art und Weise
~ of place	They play **in the park**.	~ des Ortes
~ of time	We're going to meet **at ten o'clock**.	~ der Zeit
article 10	**the/a, an**	Artikel
definite/indefinite article		bestimmter/unbestimmter Artikel
auxiliary 4	to be, to do, to have	Hilfsverb
modal auxiliary	can, may, might, must, need, should	modales Hilfsverb
substitutes for modal auxiliaries:		Ersatzformen für modale Hilfsverben
to be able to	Sarah **won't be able to** come.	
to be allowed to	Tim **is not allowed to** go outside.	
to have to	**Do** you really **have to** leave?	
comparative	ol**der**, **more** beautiful, etc.	Komparativ, 1. Steigerungsform
comparison of adjectives	small, small**er**, small**est**	Steigerung der Adjektive
comparison of adverbs	slowly, more/most slowly	Steigerung der Adverbien
comparison with more/most	**more/most** expensive	Steigerung mit more/most
conditional sentences 7		Bedingungssatz
conditional sentence type I	**If they leave**, we'll go with them.	
conditional sentence type II	If I **were** you, I **wouldn't stay**.	
conditional sentence type III	If I **had seen** the snake, I **would have run** away.	
conjunction/ connective	**and, or, because, when**, etc.	Konjunktion/Bindewort
contact clause 7	That's the film **I like best**.	Notwendiger Relativsatz ohne Relativpronomen
dynamic verbs 1	**to play, to run, to sing**	dynamische Verben
future		Futur
going-to future	We're **going to** have fun.	going-to-Futur
will future	It **will** be a big hit.	will-Futur
future perfect	By 6 o'clock, we'll already **have gone**.	Perfekt des Futurs
future progressive	What **will** you **be doing** this weekend?	Verlaufsform des Futurs
present progressive (to express the future)	What **are** you **doing** next Sunday?	Verlaufsform des Präsens (um das Futur auszudrücken)
simple present (timetable future)	The concert **starts** at 8.	einfaches Präsens (um das Futur auszudrücken)
gerund 7, 9	**Swimming** is fun.	Gerundium (Verb als Nomen)
	I'm tired of **waiting**.	
	He went away without **looking** back.	
to have something done	We should have our car checked again.	etw tun/machen lassen
if and when 7	**If** it rains, we'll go to the cinema.	konditionales 'wenn'
	When Grandma comes, she'll cook for us.	temporales 'wenn'
imperative	**Let's go!, Don't go outside!**	Imperativ (Befehlsform)
indirect speech 6		indirekte Rede
expressions of time	**yesterday the day before**	Zeitangaben
indirect commands, requests and advice	Our teacher **told us to listen**.	indirekte Befehle, Bitten und Ratschläge
indirect questions	She asked me **why I had left**.	indirekte Fragen
the introductory verb	**said, explained, argued, pointed out**, etc.	Einleitungsverben
indirect speech with tense shift	He said the film **was** great.	indirekte Rede mit Zeitverschiebung
indirect speech without tense shift	He says the film **is** great.	indirekte Rede ohne Zeitverschiebung
infinitive 9	**to play**	Infinitiv/Grundform
infinitive constructions	I'd like you **to look** at my picture.	Infinitivkonstruktionen
	We were the last **to arrive** at the party.	
infinitive after verbs of perception	I **saw** him **stop** infront of the bank.	Infinitiv nach Verben der Wahrnehmung
let + infinitive	My parents often **let** me **have** the car.	let + Infinitiv
make + infinitive	Our coach **makes** us **work** very hard.	make + Infinitiv

Appendix A

inversion 11	No sooner **had** I arrived than the game began.	Inversion/Satzumstellung
negative (form)	I **can't** swim. He's **not** here.	Verneinung
noun	**book, horse, tree**, etc.	Nomen/Substantiv
object	Jenny is buying **a pen**.	Objekt
one, prop-word	I like the green **one** better than the red **one**.	Stützwort *one*
passive voice 5 active and passive voice by-agent passive infinitive past perfect passive progressive forms in the passive verbs with prepositions in the passive verb with two objects in the passive (personal passive)	 The wall was built **by the Romans**. Changes will **be made**. Trees **had been planted**. A new school **is being built**. It**'s paid for** by the state. We **were given** instructions.	Passiv Aktiv und Passiv Verursacher einer Handlung Infinitiv des Passivs Plusquamperfekt des Passivs Verlaufsform des Passivs Passiv bei Verben mit Präpositionen Passiv bei Verben mit zwei Objekten
participles 7 present participle past participle participle with a subject of its own	**walked/walking**, while **getting out** of the car **singing, shouting**, etc. **done, eaten**, etc. All things **considered**, she felt quite happy.	Partizipien Partizip Präsens Partizip Perfekt Partizipien mit eigenem Subjekt
past perfect 2 past perfect passive past perfect progressive past perfect simple	One of the windows **had been broken**. They **had been singing** for over an hour. He **had** already **left** when I arrived.	Plusquamperfekt Plusquamperfekt des Passivs Verlaufsform des Plusquamperfekt einfaches Plusquamperfekt
past tense 2 simple past past progressive	I **went** to a party last night. We **were dancing** when the lights went out.	Vergangenheit einfache Vergangenheit Verlaufsform der Vergangenheit
plural	**two girls, children, men**, etc.	Plural (Mehrzahl)
possessive determiner	**my, your, his, her**, etc.	Possessivbegleiter
possessive pronoun	**mine, yours, his, ours**, etc.	Possessivpronomen
preposition	**at, on, under, in**, etc.	Präposition
present perfect present perfect progressive present perfect with for and since	We **haven't done** it yet. I**'ve been watching** the birds for a long time. I**'ve been living** in London **since** 2005.	Perfekt Verlaufsform des Perfekt Perfekt mit 'seit'
present tense 1 simple present present progressive	I often **go** to school by bus. Look, he**'s playing** football.	Präsens/ Gegenwart einfaches Präsens Verlaufsform des Präsens
pronoun object pronoun personal pronoun possessive pronoun relative pronoun	 **me, him, us**, etc. **he, she, it, we**, etc. **mine, yours, his, ours**, etc. **who/which/that/whose/whom**	Pronomen Personalpronomen im Objektfall Personalpronomen Possessivpronomen Relativpronomen
question question with prepositions question tag question word	**Are** you Rebecca? Who is Robert waiting **for**? That's nice, **isn't it**? **Who?, What?, Where?**, etc.	Frage Frage mit Präposition Bestätigungsfrage Fragewort
reported speech 6	= indirect speech	indirekte Rede
relative clauses 7 defining relative clause non-defining relative clause	Robin was the man **who helped the poor**. My aunt, **who lives in America**, is coming to stay next week.	Relativsätze notwendiger Relativsatz nicht notwendiger Relativsatz
sentence with comparison	Tim is **nicer than** his sister. He's **not as/so old as** Tom. But Tom runs **faster than** Tim.	Vergleich im Satz
singular	**a girl, an animal, one pen**, etc.	Singular (Einzahl)
stative verbs 1	**to know, to belong, to cost, to like**, etc.	Statische Verben
subject	**The book** is on the table.	Subjekt/ Satzgegenstand
superlative	old**est**, **the most** difficult	Superlativ/ 2. Steigerungsform
verb finite verb non-finite forms (infinitive, gerund, participle) 9	 He **draws** beautiful pictures. **to draw, drawing, drawn**	Verb (Vollverb) finites Verb infinite Verbform
word order		Wortstellung

A Appendix

Irregular Verbs

infinitive	simple past	past participle	German
to arise [əˈraɪz]	arose [əˈrəʊz]	arisen [əˈrɪzn]	sich erheben
to awake [əˈweɪk]	awoke [əˈwəʊk]	awoken [əˈwəʊkn]	erwachen
to be [biː]	was; were [wɒz; wɜː]	been [biːn]	sein
to bear [beə]	bore [bɔː]	borne [bɔːn]	(er)tragen
to beat [biːt]	beat [biːt]	beaten [ˈbiːtn]	besiegen, schlagen
to become [bɪˈkʌm]	became [bɪˈkeɪm]	become [bɪˈkʌm]	werden
to begin [bɪˈgɪn]	began [bɪˈgæn]	begun [bɪˈgʌn]	beginnen
to bend [bend]	bent [bent]	bent [bent]	beugen
to bet [bet]	bet [bet]	bet [bet]	wetten
to bid [bɪd]	bade [bæd; beɪd]	bidden [bɪdən]	heißen, gebieten
to bid [bɪd]	bid [bɪd]	bid [bɪd]	bieten (Auktion)
to bind [baɪnd]	bound [baʊnd]	bound [baʊnd]	binden
to bite [baɪt]	bit [bɪt]	bitten [ˈbɪtn]	beißen
to bleed [bliːd]	bled [bled]	bled [bled]	bluten
to blow [bləʊ]	blew [bluː]	blown [bləʊn]	blasen
to break [breɪk]	broke [brəʊk]	broken [ˈbrəʊkn]	brechen
to breed [briːd]	bred [bred]	bred [bred]	brüten, züchten
to bring [brɪŋ]	brought [brɔːt]	brought [brɔːt]	bringen
to broadcast [ˈbrɔːdkɑːst]	broadcast [ˈbrɔːdkɑːst]	broadcast [ˈbrɔːdkɑːst]	senden (TV, Radio)
to build [bɪld]	built [bɪlt]	built [bɪlt]	bauen
to burn [bɜːn]	burned; burnt [bɜːnd; bɜːnt]	burnt [bɜːnd; bɜːnt]	brennen
to burst [bɜːst]	burst [bɜːst]	burst [bɜːst]	bersten, platzen
to buy [baɪ]	bought [bɔːt]	bought [bɔːt]	kaufen
to cast [kɑːst]	cast [kɑːst]	cast [kɑːst]	werfen, (Metall) gießen
to catch [kætʃ]	caught [kɔːt]	caught [kɔːt]	fangen
to choose [tʃuːz]	chose [tʃəʊz]	chosen [ˈtʃəʊzn]	(aus)wählen
to cling [klɪŋ]	clung [klʌŋ]	clung [klʌŋ]	(sich) festhalten
to come [kʌm]	came [keɪm]	come [kʌm]	kommen
to cost [kɒst]	cost [kɒst]	cost [kɒst]	kosten
to creep [kriːp]	crept [krept]	crept [krept]	schleichen; kriechen
to cut [kʌt]	cut [kʌt]	cut [kʌt]	schneiden
to deal (with) [diːl]	dealt [delt]	dealt [delt]	(be)handeln
to dig [dɪg]	dug [dʌg]	dug [dʌg]	graben
to do [duː]	did [dɪd]	done [dʌn]	tun, machen
to draw [drɔː]	drew [druː]	drawn [drɔːn]	zeichnen
to dream [driːm]	dreamed; dreamt [driːmd; dremt]	dreamed; dreamt [driːmd; dremt]	träumen
to drink [drɪŋk]	drank [dræŋk]	drunk [drʌŋk]	trinken
to drive [draɪv]	drove [drəʊv]	driven [ˈdrɪvn]	fahren
to dwell [dwell]	dwelled; dwelt [dwelt]	dwelled; dwelt [dwelt]	(ver)weilen, wohnen
to eat [iːt]	ate [et; eɪt]	eaten [ˈiːtn]	essen
to fall [fɔːl]	fell [fel]	fallen [ˈfɔːlən]	fallen
to feed [fiːd]	fed [fed]	fed [fed]	füttern
to feel [fiːl]	felt [felt]	felt [felt]	(sich) fühlen
to fight [faɪt]	fought [fɔːt]	fought [fɔːt]	streiten, kämpfen
to find [faɪnd]	found [faʊnd]	found [faʊnd]	finden
to flee [fliː]	fled [fled]	fled [fled]	fliehen
to fling [flɪŋ]	flung [flʌŋ]	flung [flʌŋ]	schleudern
to fly [flaɪ]	flew [fluː]	flown [fləʊn]	fliegen
to forbid [fəˈbɪd]	forbade [fəˈbæd; fəˈbeɪd]	forbidden [fəˈbɪdn]	verbieten
to forecast [ˈfɔːkɑːst]	forecast [ˈfɔːkɑːst]	forecast [ˈfɔːkɑːst]	vorhersagen
to forget [fəˈget]	forgot [fəˈgɒt]	forgotten [fəˈgɒtn]	vergessen
to forgive [fəˈgɪv]	forgave [fəˈgeɪv]	forgiven [fəˈgɪvn]	vergeben, verzeihen
to freeze [friːz]	froze [frəʊz]	frozen [ˈfrəʊzn]	erstarren; gefrieren

Appendix A

infinitive	simple past	past participle	German
to get [get]	got [gɒt]	got [gɒt]; gotten (AE) [gʌtn]	(be)kommen; werden
to give [gɪv]	gave [geɪv]	given [gɪvn]	geben
to go [gəʊ]	went [went]	gone [gɒn]	gehen
to grind [graɪnd]	ground [graʊnd]	ground [graʊnd]	(zer)mahlen
to grow [grəʊ]	grew [gru:]	grown [grəʊn]	wachsen; anbauen
to hang [hæŋ]	hung [hʌŋ]	hung [hʌŋ]	hängen
to have [hæv]	had [hæd]	had [hæd]	haben
to hear [hɪə]	heard [hɜ:d]	heard [hɜ:d]	hören
to hide [haɪd]	hid [hɪd]	hidden ['hɪdn]	(sich) verstecken
to hit [hɪt]	hit [hɪt]	hit [hɪt]	schlagen; treffen
to hold [həʊld]	held [held]	held [held]	halten
to hurt [hɜ:t]	hurt [hɜ:t]	hurt [hɜ:t]	verletzen, weh tun
to keep [ki:p]	kept [kept]	kept [kept]	behalten; weitermachen
to kneel [ni:l]	knelt [nelt]	knelt [nelt]	knien
to know [nəʊ]	knew [nju:]	known [nəʊn]	wissen
to lay [leɪ]	laid [leɪd]	laid [leɪd]	legen
to lead [li:d]	led [led]	led [led]	führen
to lean [li:n]	leaned; leant [li:nd; lent]	leaned; leant [li:nd; lent]	(sich) lehnen
to leap [li:p]	leaped; leapt [li:pt; lept]	leaped; leapt [li:pt; lept]	springen
to learn [lɜ:n]	learned/learnt [lɜ:nd; lɜ:nt]	learned/learnt [lɜ:nd; lɜ:nt]	lernen
to leave [li:v]	left [left]	left [left]	(ver)lassen
to lend [lend]	lent [lent]	lent [lent]	leihen
to let [let]	let [let]	let [let]	lassen
to lie [laɪ]	lay [leɪ]	lain [leɪn]	liegen
to light [laɪt]	lit [lɪt]	lit [lɪt]	anzünden, beleuchten
to lose [lu:z]	lost [lɒst]	lost [lɒst]	verlieren
to make [meɪk]	made [meɪd]	made [meɪd]	machen
to mean [mi:n]	meant [ment]	meant [ment]	bedeuten; meinen
to meet [mi:t]	met [met]	met [met]	(sich) treffen
to mistake [mɪ'steɪk]	mistook [mɪ'stʊk]	mistaken [mɪ'steɪkn]	falsch verstehen
to mow [məʊ]	mowed [məʊd]	mowed; mown [məʊd; məʊn]	mähen
to pay [peɪ]	paid [peɪd]	paid [peɪd]	zahlen
to put [pʊt]	put [pʊt]	put [pʊt]	stellen, legen, setzen
to quit [kwɪt]	quitted; quit ['kwɪtɪd; kwɪt]	quitted; quit ['kwɪtɪd; kwɪt]	aufgeben, aufhören, verlassen
to read [ri:d]	read [red]	read [red]	lesen
to rend [rend]	rent [rent]	rent [rent]	zerreißen
to rid [rɪd]	rid [rɪd]	rid [rɪd]	loswerden, befreien (von)
to ride [raɪd]	rode [rəʊd]	ridden ['rɪdn]	reiten; fahren
to ring [rɪŋ]	rang [ræŋ]	rung [rʌŋ]	klingeln; anrufen
to rise [raɪz]	rose [rəʊz]	risen ['rɪzn]	steigen; sich erheben
to run [rʌn]	ran [ræn]	run [rʌn]	rennen, laufen
to saw [sɔ:]	sawed [sɔ:d]	sawed; sawn [sɔ:d; sɔ:n]	sägen
to say [seɪ]	said [sed]	said [sed]	sagen
to see [si:]	saw [sɔ:]	seen [si:n]	sehen
to seek [si:k]	sought [sɔ:t]	sought [sɔ:t]	suchen
to sell [sel]	sold [səʊld]	sold [səʊld]	verkaufen
to send [send]	sent [sent]	sent [sent]	schicken
to set [set]	set [set]	set [set]	setzen, legen, stellen
to sew [səʊ]	sewed [səʊd]	sewed; sewn [səʊd; səʊn]	nähen
to shake [ʃeɪk]	shook [ʃʊk]	shaken ['ʃeɪkn]	schütteln
to shed [ʃed]	shed [ʃed]	shed [ʃed]	vergießen, abwerfen
to shine [ʃaɪn]	shone [ʃɒn]	shone [ʃɒn]	scheinen, glänzen
to shoot [ʃu:t]	shot [ʃɒt]	shot [ʃɒt]	schießen
to show [ʃəʊ]	showed [ʃəʊd]	shown [ʃəʊn]	zeigen
to shrink [ʃrɪŋk]	shrank; shrunk [ʃræŋk; ʃrʌŋk]	shrunk [ʃrʌŋk]	schrumpfen, einlaufen

A Appendix

infinitive	simple past	past participle	German
to shut [ʃʌt]	shut [ʃʌt]	shut [ʃʌt]	schließen
to sing [sɪŋ]	sang [sæŋ]	sung [sʌŋ]	singen
to sink [sɪŋk]	sank [sæŋk]	sunk [sʌŋk]	sinken
to sit [sɪt]	sat [sæt]	sat [sæt]	sitzen
to slay [sleɪ]	slew [slu:]	slain [sleɪn]	erschlagen
to sleep [sli:p]	slept [slept]	slept [slept]	schlafen
to slide [slaɪd]	slid [slɪd]	slid [slɪd]	gleiten
to sling [slɪŋ]	slung [slʌŋ]	slung [slʌŋ]	schleudern, werfen
to slit [slɪt]	slit [slɪt]	slit [slɪt]	(auf)schlitzen
to smell [smel]	smelled; smelt [smeld; smelt]	smelled; smelt [smeld; smelt]	riechen
to sow [səʊ]	sowed [səʊd]	sowed; sown [səʊd; səʊn]	säen
to speak [spi:k]	spoke [spəʊk]	spoken ['spəʊkn]	sprechen
to speed [spi:d]	speeded; sped ['spi:dɪd; sped]	speeded; sped ['spi:dɪd; sped]	schnell fahren, sich beeilen
to spell [spel]	spelled; spelt [speld; spelt]	spelled; spelt [speld; spelt]	buchstabieren
to spend [spend]	spent [spent]	spent [spent]	ausgeben; verbringen
to spill [spɪl]	spilled; spilt [spɪld; spɪlt]	spilled; spilt [spɪld; spɪlt]	verschütten
to spin [spɪn]	spun; span [spʌn; spæn]	spun [spʌn]	spinnen, schnell drehen
to spit [spɪt]	spat [spæt]	spat [spæt]	spucken
to split [splɪt]	split [splɪt]	split [splɪt]	spalten
to spoil [spɔɪl]	spoiled; spoilt [spɔɪld; spɔɪlt]	spoiled; spoilt [spɔɪld; spɔɪlt]	verderben
to spread [spred]	spread [spred]	spread [spred]	(sich) verbreiten
to spring [sprɪŋ]	sprang [spræŋ]	sprung [sprʌŋ]	entspringen
to stand [stænd]	stood [stʊd]	stood [stʊd]	stehen
to steal [sti:l]	stole [stəʊl]	stolen ['stəʊln]	stehlen
to stick [stɪk]	stuck [stʌk]	stuck [stʌk]	kleben; stecken
to sting [stɪŋ]	stung [stʌŋ]	stung [stʌŋ]	stechen
to stink [stɪŋk]	stank [stæŋk]	stunk [stʌŋk]	stinken
to stride [straɪd]	strode [strəʊd]	stridden ['strɪdn]	schreiten
to strike [straɪk]	struck [strʌk]	struck [strʌk]	schlagen; anzünden
to strive [straɪv]	strove [strəʊv]	striven ['strɪvn]	streben
to swear [sweə]	swore [swɔ:]	sworn [swɔ:n]	schwören; fluchen
to sweep [swi:p]	swept [swept]	swept [swept]	fegen
to swell [swel]	swelled [sweld]	swollen ['swəʊlən]	anschwellen
to swim [swɪm]	swam [swæm]	swum [swʌm]	schwimmen
to swing [swɪŋ]	swung [swʌŋ]	swung [swʌŋ]	schwingen, schwenken
to take [teɪk]	took [tʊk]	taken ['teɪkn]	nehmen
to teach [ti:tʃ]	taught [tɔ:t]	taught [tɔ:t]	lehren
to tear [teə]	tore [tɔ:]	torn [tɔ:n]	reißen
to tell [tel]	told [təʊld]	told [təʊld]	sagen, erzählen
to think [θɪŋk]	thought [θɔ:t]	thought [θɔ:t]	denken
to thrive [θraɪv]	thrived; throve [θraɪvd; θrəʊv]	thrived; thriven [θraɪvd; 'θrɪvn]	gedeihen
to throw [θrəʊ]	threw [θru:]	thrown [θrəʊn]	werfen
to thrust [θrʌst]	thrust [θrʌst]	thrust [θrʌst]	stoßen
to tread [tred]	trod [trɒd]	trod; trodden [trɒd; 'trɒdn]	treten
to understand [ˌʌndə'stænd]	understood [ˌʌndə'stʊd]	understood [ˌʌndə'stʊd]	verstehen
to wake [weɪk]	woke [wəʊk]	woken ['wəʊkn]	aufwachen; wecken
to wear [weə]	wore [wɔ:]	worn [wɔ:n]	tragen, anhaben
to weave [wi:v]	weaved; wove [wi:vd; wəʊv]	woven ['wəʊvn]	weben
to weep [wi:p]	wept [wept]	wept [wept]	weinen
to win [wɪn]	won [wʌn]	won [wʌn]	gewinnen
to wind [waɪnd]	wound [waʊnd]	wound [waʊnd]	wickeln, aufziehen
to wring [rɪŋ]	wrung [rʌŋ]	wrung [rʌŋ]	auswringen, umdrehen
to write [raɪt]	wrote [rəʊt]	written ['rɪtn]	schreiben